Islington Chapels

Islington Chapels

An architectural guide to Nonconformist and
Roman Catholic places of worship in the London
Borough of Islington

Philip Temple

Survey of London
Royal Commission on the Historical Monuments of England

Published by the Royal Commission on the Historical Monuments of England,
Fortress House, 23 Savile Row, London W1X 2JQ

© Crown copyright 1992

First published 1992

ISBN 1 873592 06 X

British Library Cataloguing in Publication Data
A CIP catalogue record for this book is available from the British Library

Designed by Kirsty Cook, Chimæra Creative Services, 7 The Mountlands,
Hardwick Square South, Buxton SK17 6QD

Printed by BAS Printers Ltd, Stockbridge

Contents

Chairman's Preface

Nonconformist chapels and Roman Catholic churches have long received less attention from architectural historians than their Anglican counterparts. Churches and chapels of obvious importance excepted, there has, until recent years, been little systematic recording of more modest buildings which, nevertheless, add much to the character of their localities.

The Royal Commission has already recorded Nonconformist chapels and meeting-houses throughout England up to 1914, with particular stress laid upon those built before 1850. Inventory volumes have been published on *Nonconformist Chapels and Meeting-houses in Central England* (1986) and *Nonconformist Chapels and Meeting-houses in South-West England* (1991). The scope of the present book is somewhat different, though complementary. Roman Catholic churches are included, the buildings considered are predominantly post-1850, and no cut-off date has been applied.

The recording of particular classes of building within defined areas has become central to the Royal Commission's programme of architectural investigation. Increasingly, attention has been paid to those threatened by change of use or demolition. This book is the first to result from such a survey in London. It has been undertaken by the Survey of London, whose principal work remains the compilation of topographical and architectural histories of the London parishes and studies of individual buildings of importance.

Over the past decade, churches and chapels of all denominations have been subject to unprecedented threat, as falling attendances, rising costs and inflated land values have brought about closure and redevelopment or conversion to new uses. London has been particularly affected. Few Nonconformist and Roman Catholic places of worship are listed buildings, and to monitor and assess the process of change is difficult. In the case of Nonconformist chapels, the absence of any overall administrative body, and the large number of chapels erected, many of which have been given up by their original congregations, can make even their identification problematic. Any attempt at comparative judgement is complicated by the differing liturgical requirements and tastes of individual sects. Roman Catholic churches are readily identifiable, but since Alexander Rottmann's *London Catholic Churches* (1926) there has been no published attempt at a comprehensive gazetteer of Roman Catholic churches in London.

It was with this in mind that a survey of places of Christian worship outside the Established Church was suggested to the Royal Commission by English Heritage (London Division) in 1989. The Borough of Islington was chosen for study as exemplifying the varied character of much of Greater London.

Islington has a strong tradition of Protestant Nonconformity and a large Roman Catholic population of long standing. An area of intense building activity in the 19th century, with many new communities formed, it contained districts of great poverty, and this combination proved attractive to ministers and missionaries of all persuasions. The architectural legacy of their zeal remains considerable.

As well as great monuments such as Wesley's Chapel, Islington contains numerous lesser churches, chapels and mission halls, many of which have been remodelled to suit changing needs or adapted to secular uses. Scores more have disappeared as a result of bombing, redevelopment, fire or decay. It is hoped that this book will draw attention to the continuing destruction of such buildings, not only in Islington but throughout London and elsewhere, and help to promote the understanding and appreciation of those that remain.

PARK OF MONMOUTH

Commissioners

Foreword

Islington Chapels describes places of Christian worship in the London Borough of Islington other than those built for the Established Church. It covers chapels, churches, meeting-houses and mission halls built for what are broadly known as Protestant Nonconformist churches, including non-denominational bodies, and for the Roman Catholic Church (excluding pre-Reformation churches).

It is based on field recording and documentary research carried out from 1989 to 1991 by the RCHME, initially at the suggestion of English Heritage (London Division). The main purpose of the book is to draw attention to such buildings generally and encourage appreciation of their architecture and local significance.

The London Borough of Islington was formed in 1965 from the Metropolitan Boroughs of Islington and Finsbury. The former covered the civil parish of St Mary, Islington, the latter those of St Luke, Finsbury, and St James, Clerkenwell. Islington, Finsbury and Clerkenwell each have their own religious traditions, and to a great extent still retain separate identities both socially and topographically. The distinction is greatest between Islington, north of Pentonville Road and City Road, and the area to the south, comprising Clerkenwell and Finsbury. Pentonville, north of Pentonville Road, is within Clerkenwell parish, but has a closer affinity with Islington than the rest of Clerkenwell.

The distinction between Clerkenwell and Finsbury is less apparent. Charles Booth, in his survey *Life and Labour of the People in London*, regarded Central Street as the boundary between the two districts, well to the east of the parochial boundary.

It should be kept in mind that the colloquial use of borough, parish and district names is often vague or incorrect. Part of what is often termed Finsbury, including Finsbury Circus, is in the City of London, and part of Shoreditch, in the London Borough of Hackney, is sometimes referred to as Finsbury. The name Pentonville is often used to refer incorrectly to the district around Pentonville Prison, which is actually Barnsbury.

The terms 'evangelism' and 'evangelical' also call for some explanation. 'Evangelism' has been taken to refer to the act of spreading the gospel and to proselytic Christianity of all persuasions. 'Evangelical' has been used to describe evangelistic Protestant denominations generally, including the Evangelical party of the Established Church.

The terms 'church', 'chapel', and to a lesser extent 'meeting-house', are more problematic. No hard-and-fast rule can easily be applied to their use. 'Chapel' began to replace 'meeting-house' in the 18th century, largely through its use by Methodists. Methodist usage implied a place of worship subsidiary to a parish church. But as Methodism diverged from the Established Church and other Nonconformists took up the word, 'chapel' was applied to many Nonconformist meeting-houses, though not to those of sects, notably the Quakers, who do not practise any sacraments and whose buildings therefore have no sanctuary.

The term 'church', long in use by Presbyterians, was adopted by many Congregationalists and Unitarians by the late 19th century. The word 'chapel', having acquired pejorative social connotations, is used less and less by Nonconformist congregations today. Architecturally, the various terms can only usefully be distinguished in a particular historical and denominational context.

The book is in three main parts. The first part considers some important religious and architectural developments. The religious backgrounds in the respective parishes of Islington, Clerkenwell and Finsbury are outlined, and the interaction of religion with changing social conditions is discussed. Some consideration is also given to the reasons for the decline of evangelism and chapel-building in the 20th century. The main architectural developments are traced, with particular reference to local examples, from the earliest purpose-built meeting-houses to present-day churches.

The second part is a descriptive gazetteer of existing buildings, arranged alphabetically by street within postal districts. It should be noted that parts of some postal districts fall outside the borough boundary and that the borough boundary, not the postal district, is the criterion for inclusion (Maberly Chapel in the London Borough of Hackney is included for historical reasons). The Listed Building status of buildings, where applicable, is also given.

The third section comprises notes on demolished places of worship, arranged alphabetically by street. A list of architects and their work falling within the scope of this book is appended. A select list of sources used in the compilation of the book, a glossary of names and denominations and the file number of each building in the National Buildings Record are also given.

Acknowledgements

The investigation of buildings, documentary research and writing of the text were carried out in 1989–91 by Philip Temple, under the editorship of Hermione Hobhouse, General Editor, Survey of London. Temporary research assistance was given by Martha Goodell and Caragh Wells. The buildings were photographed by Derek Kendall, who was also responsible for the documentary photography. The photographs were printed by Mike Seaforth. The plans of buildings and the map are the work of Ron New of the Survey of London. Other Royal Commission staff and Commissioners who gave valuable help and advice were John Bold, Bridget Cherry, Derek Keene and Christopher Stell (consultant to the Royal Commission). Design and production were overseen by Kate Owen, Managing Editor. Outside the Royal Commission, copy editing was undertaken by Susan Leiper.

The Royal Commission gratefully acknowledges the help of the following institutions and individuals during the preparation of this book: Philippa Boardman; British Library; British Newspaper Library; Corporation of London Records Office; Diocese of Westminster Parish Buildings Section; Dr Williams's Library; John Ellis; English Heritage (London Division); Evangelical Library; Denis Evinson; Finsbury Library (London Borough of Islington); Greater London History Library (Corporation of London); Greater London Record Office (Corporation of London); Guildhall Library (Corporation of London); Ruth Guilding; Eric Holdstock; Islington Central Library (London Borough of Islington); London Borough of Islington Building Control Department; Museum of Methodism; Public Record Office; Royal Institute of British Architects Library and Drawings Collection; Society of Friends Library; Swedenborgian Society Library; United Reformed Church Historical Society; Victorian Society.

In addition, thanks are due to the many ministers, priests, church officials, custodians and other individuals, whose help in providing information and allowing access to buildings and archives was invaluable.

Introduction

Evangelism in Islington

The evangelical background

'Islington,' said a writer on 'Holloway Fervour' in 1875, '…is proverbially referred to as the hot-bed of evangelicalism.'[1]

There was in late Victorian Islington a variety of forms of Christian worship as wide as anywhere in London. But it was predominantly evangelistic. Missions abounded. 1875 was the year that the American evangelists Moody and Sankey descended on London. Their huge meetings at the Royal Agricultural Hall in Upper Street reinforced the already strong association in the public mind of Islington with 'revival'.

As the Evangelical movement in the Established Church weakened in the late 19th century, Nonconformist churches took over. Throughout North London, concluded the *Daily News* religious survey of 1902–3, 'Nonconformity leads and the Church of England follows – but follows slowly.'[2] Nonconformist influence on evangelical Anglicanism at this time is exemplified by the future Bishop of Chelmsford, John Watts-Ditchfield, who ran a highly evangelical curacy at St Peter's, Dartmouth Park Hill, in the 1890s. Once a Wesleyan preacher, he had trained as a Wesleyan overseas missionary and it was in the wake of his failure to be posted abroad that he came to Upper Holloway.

From mid-century to turn-of-the-century, Nonconformist church attendances in the parish of Islington rose from barely a third of the total to more than half. South of City Road, in Finsbury and Clerkenwell, the Nonconformist lead was even more marked. By 1903 there were twenty Anglican places of worship in the Borough of Finsbury, none well attended, including three missions which were 'So far as numbers go…a complete failure'.[3] In contrast, three Baptist churches regularly drew more than a thousand worshippers each.

Outside mainstream Nonconformity, the Swedenborgians waged 'active propaganda amongst those…dissatisfied with the teachings of other sects'.[4] The Roman Catholic Church, too, was active in proselytization. By the early 20th century more than half the regular congregation at St Joseph's, Highgate Hill, were said to be converts.

Behind all this activity were long-standing local traditions, stemming from the Established and Dissenting churches. The three parishes making up the present borough – Finsbury, Clerkenwell and Islington – each made distinct contributions to this overall picture of evangelical zeal.

Conveniently proximate to the City, Finsbury had been a centre of Dissent since the 17th century. It contained the Quaker cemetery where George Fox was buried and the Dissenters' *campo santo* at Bunhill Fields. More important still was Finsbury's connection with the rise of Wesleyan and Calvinistic Methodism in the mid-18th century.

In 1739 John Wesley and George Whitefield preached at Moorfields, Wesley in a ruined gun foundry, Whitefield standing on a table by a brick wall. The 'Foundery' was repaired and opened as the first Methodist preaching-house in London. It became the headquarters of a mission whose services included a medical dispensary and a refuge for widows and children. Nearby, Whitefield's followers built the 'Tabernacle', to which a remarkable cross-section of the intelligentsia and aristocracy – including Walpole, Hogarth, Hume, Franklin, Sarah, Duchess of Marlborough, and the Duke of Cumberland – came to hear him preach.

Whitefield's Tabernacle (rebuilt 1753 and 1868) fell into decline, but the Foundery and its successor, Wesley's Chapel, remained an important focus for evangelism.

Clerkenwell too had a strong evangelical tradition. It also had a tradition of political radicalism, free-thinking and atheism. There were links with the early Quakers, through Peel Court Meeting-house, and with the Countess of Huntingdon's Connexion. The Countess herself lived next door to Spa Fields Chapel, which she opened and which became one of the leading Dissenting chapels in London. In 1788 Spa Fields Chapel provided the first minister for Pentonville Chapel.

Another influential local figure was Emanuel Swedenborg (1688–1772), who lived in Clerkenwell for some years until his death. Robert Hindmarsh (1759–1835), the founder of the Swedenborgian New Church, was a Clerkenwell printer. One of the first New Church 'temples' was built for Hindmarsh in 1796–7 just outside the parish, in Hatton Garden, the society meeting there later moving to Camden Road, Upper Holloway. The Hatton Garden chapel was used by the Revd Edward Irving during the genesis of the Catholic Apostolic Church.

Congregationalists had an old-established base at Claremont Chapel, Pentonville. But as in Finsbury, it was Wesleyan Methodism which, during the late Victorian period, dominated the evangelical scene with its highly organized missionary work.

In the parish of Islington, evangelicalism did not become strong until much later than in Finsbury and Clerkenwell. When it did so, it was mainly associated with the Established Church and Independents (Congregationalists). Whitefield and the Wesleys were invited to preach at Islington parish church in the late 1730s, resulting in a row which led to the vicar's departure and set back local evangelicalism at that time. Not until the building of Union Chapel in 1806 did evangelicalism take root. Founded by Independents, Union Chapel was set up 'as the friend of *all* – free, and open for the occasional labours of Evangelical Ministers of the Church of England, the Church of Scotland, and those who dissent from them'.[5]

The induction of Daniel Wilson (1788–1858) as Vicar of Islington in 1824 presaged an evangelical drive. That year, the Church Missionary Society (CMS) set up its college in Upper Street, the first seminary in the country for Anglican missionaries. In 1828 Wilson formed a local group to assist the CMS: 'From that time Islington became a missionary parish.'[6] When Wilson departed for India in 1832 as the Bishop of Calcutta, he left a secure evangelical legacy. The patronage of several daughter churches was in the vicar's hands, and the living itself – the advowson was purchased by Wilson's uncle for £5,500 in 1811 – was in the gift of an evangelical trust. The Islington Clerical Meetings, annual conferences inaugurated by Wilson, proved enduring and played a key role in promoting Islington's evangelical reputation.

As well as the CMS college, which flourished until 1915, Islington became the home of other important theological and evangelical establishments, both within and without the Established Church.

Highbury College, opened in 1826, trained aspiring Congregationalist ministers. In 1850 it transferred to Hampstead as part of New College. The premises were sold to the Metropolitan Church of England Training Institution. They were acquired in 1866 by the evangelical London School of Divinity as an Anglican theological college, which became part of the University of London in 1934.

Pre-eminent among local missions was the undenominational Mildmay Mission, started c1860 in Barnet by the vicar, the Revd William Pennefather, and based at Mildmay Park from 1864. Widely influential, it spawned many evangelical and social organizations. It was to be near the Mildmay Mission that Hudson Taylor of the China Inland Mission set up headquarters at 6 Pyrland Road in 1872 (later moving to new premises at 45 Newington Green).

By the turn of the century the most successful churches in Islington were Congregational, and their influence was much felt by Anglicans. All Saints', Holloway, was particularly 'Congregationalist'. Congregationalism was a largely middle-class persuasion. Baptist churches attracted a higher proportion of working-class members, but were comparatively under-attended and did less missionary work. The Salvation Army, drawing its ranks largely from the working class, was also active. Methodists did nothing in the parish to match the 'feverish excitement'[7] with which the youth-oriented Leysian Mission set to work in the slums of Finsbury. In the inter-war years Methodists became more energetic locally, opening two central halls – the last big mission halls to be built in Islington.

The social context

Social conditions in Victorian Islington provided a fertile breeding-ground for any number of sects and missions, competing with each other and against the rival attractions of pubs, prostitutes and music-halls for the attention of a predominantly working-class and lower-middle-class populace. But in practice the mass of the working class was unaffected, being indifferent to religion. Evangelists concentrated their efforts on the poorest, who could not always afford to be indifferent.

In Finsbury and Clerkenwell, where poverty was widespread, large missions provided education and welfare as well as spreading the gospel. In the parish of Islington, where poverty was much more localized and the middle-class population was larger, smaller missions were active, connected with neighbouring, mostly middle-class, congregations.

Today, after much demolition and rebuilding, a pattern of 18th- and 19th-century chapel-building is still traceable, radiating from the oldest built-up centres. Congregational chapels, spreading north, east and west of the area round Islington parish church, mark the advance of middle-class colonization during a century, from the building of Islington Chapel in 1788 to the building of Highbury Quadrant Congregational Church in 1881–2. Wesley's Chapel and Whitefield Tabernacle recall the affluent residential character of part of Finsbury. In Clerkenwell, Pentonville Chapel (rebuilt as Grimaldi Park House) and a concentration of early 19th-century chapels reflect the development of middle-class housing in the northern part of the parish.

Chapel-building accompanied house-building, diversity of denomination reflecting the diverse backgrounds of the newcomers. Sizeable ethnic minorities, particularly the Welsh, built their own chapels. Mission halls followed a more wayward path, determined partly by house-building of the meaner sort, but more often by changes in the social character of old built-up areas.

Underlying the spread of both chapels and missions were the steady growth and movement of the population. In the parish of Islington the population rose from 15,000 in 1811 to 320,000 in 1891. The fastest period of growth was in the 1840s–70s. By the late 19th century Islington was almost completely built up and was experiencing at a growing pace the progressive social deterioration of hitherto genteel localities, a phenomenon long evident in Clerkenwell and Finsbury.

The centrifugal movement of the population, affecting the whole of London to a greater or lesser degree, was, until post-war gentrification partly reversed the process, the leading factor in causing changes in social character: 'Those who come are poorer than those who go, and each district in turn grows poorer...The outward impulse extends to the extreme North, where the poorest and worst, in their desire for cheaper houses or less stringent rules, cross the London boundary, as do the rich in search of pleasant gardens and green fields.'[8]

Population movement and its concomitants constantly threw down challenges for churches and missions. The positive aspects were many: municipal improvements, slum clearance and housing schemes, commercial development, the creation of entire suburbs. But the corollary was multiple occupancy of property elsewhere, more crime and prostitution, inner-city decay. With social deterioration came religious decline, affecting all denominations:

> The Nonconformists are not a whit more successful than the Church...their regular chapels are all empty, and the result of their mission work is small. Several of the chapels, that prospered here 'while the shopkeepers still lived over their shops'...have been entirely closed. Their place is taken by special missions, connected, in most cases, with an active church elsewhere. With these missions the regular working class will have nothing to do. The poor and degraded are sought, and for them 'a great deal is done with small results'.[9]

In late 19th-century Islington the unequivocally wealthy were confined to an enclave comprising Highbury New Park, Aberdeen Park and the southern parts of Highbury Quadrant and Highbury Hill. Most of Highbury was middle and lower middle class, shading into poorer neighbourhoods in Highbury Vale and Finsbury Park. To the south, Canonbury was middle class and a middle-class belt extended along Upper Street. A large middle-class quarter surrounded Holloway Prison, in the area of Tufnell Park and Camden Road.

Much of Tollington Park, Lower Holloway, Barnsbury and the Essex Road area were mixed working class and lower middle class. Pentonville contained widespread poverty. Scattered pockets of penury included areas around Gifford Street and Brewery Road south of the Metropolitan Cattle Market, George's Road and Hampden Road off Holloway Road, Queensland Road off Hornsey Road, and Britannia Row off Essex Road.

In Clerkenwell and Finsbury were a few middle-class strongholds, such as Lloyd Square and Myddelton Square. Poor areas were interspersed more thickly than in the north among comparatively well-off parts, but many slums had already been cleared and the process was continuing.

Close to the City, in Clerkenwell and Finsbury, the early pattern of development had, by the mid-18th century, become fossilized in a matrix of accretive building. Street frontages and off-street footpaths were built up; gardens were built over. Where it survived, the resulting amalgam produced some of the worst slum conditions of Victorian London. Impenetrable to the police, chronically insanitary, these rookeries absorbed the poorest and most desperate. Rife with vice and irreligion, they were irresistible to missionaries.

Whitefield's Tabernacle in Moorfields was so-called in appropriate allusion to the Tabernacle of the Israelites in the Wilderness. Although much of Finsbury was already densely built up, the east and north was largely open, a place of ponds, tenter-grounds,[10] graveyards and the dog-kennels of the Lord Mayor's Hunt. The wall by which Whitefield had preached in 1739 was razed when locals complained to the City Corporation of 'Thieves Sodomites & other Dangerous and Wicked Persons continually lurking & secreting themselves' under it at night: '...many Robberies have of late been committed there & other ill practices carried on to the great Hazard & Peril of persons whose business obliges them to pass...the greatest indecencies are committed even in the daytime...'[11]

The making of City Road in 1761 and the development of Finsbury Square from 1777 to 1792 provided houses for the well-to-do, but most of Finsbury remained poor and crowded. Notorious warrens along Golden Lane early attracted the attention of missionaries. Radnor Street Mission, connected with Wesley's Chapel, originated in a Sunday school founded in Golden Lane in 1798. The 19th century saw a number of missions active in the area, including the Golden Lane Mission to Costermongers, founded in 1862 by W. J. Orsman, a friend of Lord Shaftesbury. By the early 20th century most of the middle class had gone and Finsbury had 'fallen on evil times': 'Poverty pervades. Vice is resident and regnant. There is no natural or artificial beauty anywhere, no sight to soften the dismal dirtiness, no sound to alleviate the depressing misery of its vice...St. Luke is as noted for its thieves as Clerkenwell is for its watches...the worst criminal quarter in London...'[12]

Because of this long history of poverty, few chapels were built in Finsbury. There were several large missions, but in an area where conditions of life (notably around Central Street) reportedly fell below even those of Hoxton, more might have been expected. The explanation probably lies in Finsbury's lack of cachet in the eyes of potential benefactors. As an Anglican at St Mary's, Golden Lane, complained: 'We are not the East End.'[13] The most important missions – the Leysian Mission and the Quakers' adult schools – had origins long ago. There was a go-getting mission of purely Victorian provenance at Great Arthur Street Baptist Chapel, in the heart of the slums between Golden Lane and Goswell Road. It was run by the Revd Reuben May, incomparable practitioner of 'the begging art': 'Mr. May and his family live by the mission…and the money spent on themselves may be as well, and indeed is probably better spent than that which goes towards the indiscriminate feeding of the people, which is the backbone of this mission work and the sole secret of the attendance of large numbers of the homeless poor, both on Sundays and week-days, at the religious services.'[14]

Clerkenwell too harboured many destitute. Writing in 1852, a former London City Missionary described 'grovelling, starving poverty' in a Clerkenwell infested by thieves and receivers, where 'brazen, ragged women scream and shout ribald repartees from window to window'. He recounted a visit to a family in a Clerkenwell alley: 'I found the husband, who had long been out of work, gnawing something black, and inquired what it was; he…said it was a bone he had picked off a dunghill, and charred in the fire…These people were *actually* starving, and had been without food for two days.'[15]

In parts of Pentonville squalor was endemic. A report of 1859 told of conditions in a court off what is now Chapel Market. On Sundays the water supply from the single standpipe was stopped, and the inhabitants used a well in the undrained yard where costermongers buried rotting food and which was feet deep in 'slime and filth'.[16] By the late 19th century many of the worst slums had been cleared, but some remained well into the 20th century.

Missions of all persuasions grappled with the problems engendered by such deprivation. Among the oldest missions active in Clerkenwell was the Field Lane Institution, founded in 1841, based just over the parish bounds in Vine Street (now Vine Hill). It ran refuges, ragged schools, a crèche, and (in Hampstead) children's industrial homes. There were Sunday services for tramps. Lured by cocoa, most comers were cynical or apathetic. As a religious influence, the Institution's value was 'probably extremely small'; its social value possibly 'a minus quantity'.[17]

The leading Nonconformist venture was the Wesleyan London Central Mission at St John's Square Methodist Chapel. Built in 1849, by the 1880s the church was virtually redundant, the congregation 'a mere handful of folk whose slender means compelled them to remain in the district'.[18] The new mission flung itself into the work of salvation with preaching, Sunday schools, temperance meetings, brass bands, and a range of activities including a 'Public-House Brigade' and a Bible class in connection with the Christian Policemen's Association.

Analysing 'The Problem of North London' in 1904, Walter R. Warren described Islington as a place of squalid overcrowding where the well-to-do and middle classes were in retreat before an influx of working people and the borough was daily 'becoming more a caravanserai of ever-shifting lodgers'.

> No one can fail to observe it. Whether one alights from a 'bus at the Angel and penetrates the backs of High Street and Upper Street, or travels in and out of the side streets branching off the Caledonian Road…or along the Seven Sisters Road – it is both real and certain that poverty, vice, and low life are there, potent with evil and pitiful to the last degree.[19]

Low life was there, but localized. Campbell Road, 'the worst street in North London'[20] was in a largely respectable district off Seven Sisters Road:

> A street fairly broad, with houses of three storeys, not ill-built, many being occupied as common lodging houses; broken windows, dirty curtains, doors open, a litter of paper, old meat tins, heads of fish and stalks of vegetables. It is a street where thieves and prostitutes congregate. The thieves live in the common lodging-houses, paying 4d. a night, and the prostitutes, generally two together, in a single furnished room, which they rent at four or five shillings a week. They are the lowest class of back street prostitute, and an hour or two after midnight they may be seen returning home.[21]

At least some residents were migrants cleared from slum districts to the south. Others came from the country, the men navvying on building sites and railways and generally turning to drink rather than religion.

Bad as things were at the turn of the century from the missionaries' point of view, there had been plenty to criticise in the past – fondly though it might be recalled by some. Warren himself (plagiarizing Thornbury's *Old and New London*) sighed for a lost 'Merrie Islington' of the 18th century: 'Where is now that Highbury Barn, so noted for its ale and cakes; or Cream Hall, whereat our grandsires gathered, hot and dusty, on a shining summer afternoon, to quaff new milk, eat custards cool, and cakes delicious, dipped in frothing cream?'[22]

Highbury Barn had been pulled down some thirty years earlier, a victim of genteel disapproval by affluent locals of the dancing, drinking and diverse amusements for which it was famed. Censure of Islington's character as a popular resort went back to the early days of local evangelicalism. Robert Cowie, who lived near Highbury Barn and helped found Union Chapel, recalled late 18th-century Islington as 'in a state of religious destitution'.

> The grossest ignorance and immorality prevailed…The tea gardens and public houses were the places of Sabbath resort for thousands of gay and dissipated characters from the neighbouring Metropolis. Tradesmen were seen carrying on their usual traffic in shops, either wholly open on the Lord's Day, or paying a grudging hypocritical homage to its claims by putting up half their window-shutters, vainly attempting to serve God and Mammon.[23]

By the late 19th century this attitude was giving way to a sense of guilt:

> Whilst we have been building our churches and solacing ourselves with our religion and dreaming that the millennium was coming, the poor have

been growing poorer, and the wretched more miserable, and the immoral more corrupt. The gulf has been daily widening which separates the lowest classes of the community from our churches and chapels, and from all decency and civilisation.[24]

While it was easy enough to condemn vice and drink in streets such as Campbell Road, over wider areas it was obvious that any immorality to be fought was not simply that of the inhabitants. Barnsbury, for instance, contained much social iniquity. A report on the sanitary condition of the streets between Caledonian Road and York Way in 1863 described a one-room tenement there:

> …we found a child dead from scarlet fever; another ill of the same complaint; no washing had been done for a fortnight, and the clothes which had been worn by the sick child, and those which had been taken off the dead one, were stowed in the bottom of a cupboard, where the food of the family was kept: there were dirty slops in the room and on the staircase; and the door and window were but too carefully closed; in fact, we were told that the window had never been opened… The woman who lived here had buried three children, and the one lying dead was the fourth lost, while the only one surviving was not likely to live. The other rooms in the house were crowded; the drainage was not good; and two other children had died in the same place not long before…[25]

The same report detailed the ill-ventilated basement school of a nearby chapel (probably Caledonian Road Congregational Chapel), popular as it had a good educational reputation – despite charging 6d per child a week, double the National School rate. Part had been partitioned off to form 'a small box' for more than eighty infants; they sat on a gallery, 'row above row…packed close together, like oranges in a chest…'

The condition of the district did not altogether improve. Twenty-five years later, most of this area, north of Bingfield Street, was still characterized by 'chronic want'.[26] After the Second World War, Harold Clunn found Barnsbury 'funereal and depressing' and Caledonian Road 'a most squalid thoroughfare of long drab terraces of three-storeyed houses and poverty-stricken shops, none of which it would seem, have ever been cleaned or decorated'.[27] In the late 1950s, F. H. Wrintmore of the London City Mission found the area a place of 'squalor, monotonous depravity, physical and structural decay…a vacuum of despair: a deathly *cul-de-sac*'.[28]

But although some of the social problems that had been such a magnet to missionaries remained, the great days of evangelism were well over by the Second World War. Chapel-building had long gone out of fashion; so had 'revival' itself.

The decline of evangelism

Islington Chapel (opened 1815) had a long history of schism. In its early years the congregation had little say in its running and the Anglican liturgy was used. In 1827 a new minister introduced the Independent form of service, splitting the congregation, and left to set up Barnsbury Chapel nearby. By 1840, when the Revd Benjamin Hollis took over, membership was low. It rose, despite dissension, but then Hollis attempted to restore the old-style government and liturgy, suggesting that anyone who disagreed should leave. Some did, but ill-feeling simmered and he was later forced out, 'partly from his desire to restore the old government by himself alone, but still more from rumours against his character, & not a little to his having married unhappily'.[29]

In 1899 the publication of a novel by the daughter of the pastor of Providence Baptist Chapel led to his resignation; the story was too close to home for some members of the 'shabby little chapel'.[30]

Such liturgical and personal disputes did nothing to strengthen the churches against the growing secularization of society at large. Long before the Second World War, a combination of forces had undermined their position.

The northern drift of the population was only one factor – which, sometimes, was turned to apparent advantage. From at least as early as the 1870s, conversion to mission status offered hope of new life to moribund chapels. In 1872 Pentonville Road Congregational Church hoped that Union Chapel would take over their premises as a mission. In 1893, in the face of chronic financial and membership problems, Claremont Chapel was offered to the London Congregational Union as a mission station.

The evolution of the welfare state reduced the need for, and undermined the theoretical basis of, the social subvention offered by missionaries.[31] Slum clearance and municipal improvements blunted the poignancy of how the poor lived. At the same time, the consciences of many members of the middle classes were eased by their own falling standards of living. State schools helped to bring about the long-term decline of religious involvement in education. Cinema eclipsed church hall lantern slide lectures. Innumerable social developments, while not necessarily anti-religious, had the effect of promoting secularization.

The largely 19th-century infrastructure of churches, chapels and missions remained substantially intact until the Second World War. After the war, many bombed churches were not reinstated. Others finally closed after weathering decades of decline.

Chapel- and church-building

18th-century meeting-houses: converted buildings

In the 17th and 18th centuries many Nonconformist meetings were held in private houses and other *ad hoc* premises, but the growth of settled congregations called for buildings dedicated to religious uses, whether purpose-built or converted.

St John's Church, Clerkenwell, built by the Order of St John of Jerusalem in the 12th century and sacked during the Peasants' Rebellion, became a private chapel after the Restoration. It was later used as a Presbyterian meeting-house, which it remained until wrecked during the pro-High Church Sacheverell riots in 1710.

The Foundery in Moorfields was used for casting ordnance for the government, but in 1716 damp moulds caused a devastating explosion at the attempted recasting of French cannon. It stood derelict until 1739, when Wesley leased the 'vast uncouth heap of ruins'[32] from the City Corporation, turning it into a preaching-house. The imminent expiry of the lease, disrepair and the redevelopment of the City's Finsbury Estate prompted its replacement by Wesley's Chapel, a little to the north, in 1777–8.

In 1752 Wesley reopened a failed amusement hall, the New Wells, Rosoman Street, for preaching. Spa Fields Chapel nearby also originated as a place of amusement, the Pantheon, built for a former publican in 1770. Noorthouck described it as 'an humble imitation of the *Pantheon* in Oxford-street' where 'apprentices, journeymen, and clerks, dressed to ridiculous extremes, entertain their ladies on Sundays, and...affect the dissipated manners of their superiors'. [33] Evangelizing Anglican clergymen took it over in 1777, but were hauled before the Ecclesiastical Court for preaching in an unconsecrated building. It was bought by the Countess of Huntingdon and remained in use by the Connexion until its enforced demolition more than a century later. A rotunda with galleries on two levels, it was ideal for preaching.

Later converted buildings and hired halls

Many local buildings were used at various times for religious purposes, often public halls or disused premises bought or leased by churches. Barnsbury Hall, Barnsbury Street, a mid-19th-century building now serving as a factory, was used in the 1850s and 1860s by seceders from Barnsbury Chapel. Myddelton Hall in Almeida Street and Holloway Hall in Holloway Road were regularly hired for religious meetings.

The Almeida Theatre, Almeida Street, was built as a Literary and Scientific Institute. It was later a Salvation Army Hall and a Christadelphian Church, before becoming a carnival novelty factory. The Little Angel Theatre in Dagmar Passage, built in 1849 as the parish infants' school, was for many years a temperance hall. More recently, in about 1962, commercial premises at 16A Highbury Place were converted to a Kingdom Hall for Jehovah's Witnesses. It is now the Evangelical Brotherhood Church.

Early purpose-built meeting-houses

One of the earliest purpose-built meeting-houses in the present borough was in Peel Court, Clerkenwell, a plain building of square plan built in 1721 to replace a workshop where meetings had long been held. Lower Street Meeting-house (1740) was the first built in Islington parish. Like Peel Court Meeting, it was of conventional design and 'Built in a Plain Manner'. [34]

Whitefield's Tabernacle in Moorfields, built in 1752–3 to replace a timber structure of 1741, was unusually large but equally utilitarian.

Late 18th-century and early 19th-century chapels

The first chapels, as opposed to meeting-houses, built in what is now the London Borough of Islington, were very similar to Anglican churches or chapels of ease, both in liturgical arrangement and architectural character. Unlike many earlier meeting-houses, they eschewed centralized square or octagonal plans in favour of rectangular naves with an East end, [35] sometimes containing a small sanctuary or sacrarium. They were not inconspicuous and plain, as were many meeting-houses, but were built in the fashionable style of the day.

The earliest, Wesley's Chapel (1777–8), although somewhat plain externally, was almost certainly designed by a leading Neoclassical architect. Pentonville Chapel (1787–8, later St James's, Pentonville), although built as a proprietary chapel, was always intended for Anglican use. It too was the work of a talented architect, A. H. Hurst.

Lack of funds delayed the completion of the first Islington Chapel (1788–93), in Church Street (now Gaskin Street), and its intended character is not certain. Highbury Grove Chapel (c1793), a building of some architectural pretension, closed before it was finished and reopened in 1799 as the precursor of Union Chapel. Holloway Independent Chapel was built in 1804; burned down in 1807, it was rebuilt using fittings from the conveniently defunct Highbury Grove Chapel. It had a pedimented façade in three bays with round-arched windows on two levels, typical of the more modest chapels of the late 18th and early 19th centuries.

Union Chapel (1806) a stucco-fronted Classical-style building with a cupola, had a rectangular plan with a curved East end, and was intended to be compatible with the Anglican liturgy. The work of the architect-builder Jacob Leroux, developer of Somers Town, it was built on a 99-year lease and formed the centrepiece of Compton Terrace, which he began. The financing of the building was through the issue of £100 shares. Leroux took some, but it was not a 'joint-stock' venture and there was indignation when they were misleadingly advertised for sale.

The second Islington Chapel (1814–15), in Upper Street, stuccoed and turreted, was no doubt designed with an eye on Union Chapel.

The twenty or so years before Queen Victoria's accession saw the building of many chapels in the present borough, mostly in southern Islington and Clerkenwell, several of them on the principal local estates, erected on long building leases and roughly contemporaneous with nearby house-building.

All these chapels had rectangular plans (arranged on the long axis) and symmetrical fronts. They were mostly plain and none had cupolas or turrets. Of this period, Northampton Tabernacle (now the Roman Catholic Church of SS Peter and Paul) is the most ambitious, with a well considered Italianate façade.

Gothic did not become common for chapels until the late 1840s. The first Gothic Revival chapels locally were the Tudor-style Free-Thinking Christians' meeting-house (1832) in St John's Square, Clerkenwell, and the Scottish Presbyterian church (1834) in Colebrooke Row.

Victorian chapels

There was an enormous growth in chapel-building during the second half of the 19th century. It was fuelled by population increase and urban and suburban development. But chapel-building became a fashion rather than a necessity. Chapels were often built in a burst of confidence without adequate regard for practical considerations. Numerous chapels were much too large for their congregations, too expensive to maintain, or were designed in styles which soon went out of date. Some were downright shoddy. Consequently, many chapels became a burden and an embarrassment to later generations of worshippers, a fact which has encouraged much adverse criticism and helped to give the word 'chapel' disparaging connotations in some quarters.

Contemporary criticism of Victorian chapels often ignored the fact that the liturgical requirements of most Nonconformist congregations were different to those of Anglicans, however Low: 'The architect's ingenuity seems to expend itself at the outset; and after the turrets and gables of the front, we come to the inevitable barn that lies behind.'[36]

But barn-like chapels of rectangular plan were cheap to build, providing the simplest means of accommodating the maximum of worshippers with a clear view of the preacher. They were well suited to urban sites, particularly in terraces, where street frontage was at a premium. High, open roofs made possible the installation of galleries which in a flat-ceilinged building would have been intolerably stuffy or demanded considerably higher walls. It was a type of building which naturally called for Gothic or Romanesque style, but was at odds with Gothic Revival ideals as they developed during the mid- to late 19th century. It was the willingness of Nonconformist architects to perpetuate increasingly despised Anglican prototypes that was particularly resented:

> There was a time...when churches were built 'in the Gothic taste' with huge barn-like roofs, side windows cut in half by a gallery, and miserable caricatures of tower and pinnacle to form a 'front.' The meanest church would shrink from such barbarisms now, but many an 'elegant and commodious' chapel affords them a refuge. It used to be thought...that the spirit of mediaevalism abhorred all ceilings, except vaulted ones: that it must be propitiated by high open roofs, no matter how wiry...how bad acoustically, how good as conductors of heat and cold; that it delighted in angles, breaks and diminutive buttresses...these were the mistakes of more than twenty years ago. The mass of chapel architecture seems to follow the world at twenty years' distance...'[37]

These characteristics are evident at Henry Hodge's Congregational church, Pentonville Road (1857, now King's Cross Welsh Tabernacle). The diminutive tower and pinnacles have gone, but the barn-like interior with windows bisected by the gallery remain. In an earlier scheme for the site, Hodge proposed a chapel with a roof so open that the Metropolitan Building Office took exception: 'We look with alarm at yr roof. No tie; no collar –'.[38]

The low budgets on which chapels were often built exacerbated the problem of flimsiness at a time when Gothic Revival architects were emphasising solidity of construction. Hodge's Welsh Calvinistic Methodist chapel in Wilton Square (1852–3) caused the Metropolitan Building Office concern on account of the slightness of the roof and the inadequate support given to overhanging turrets at the gable ends. It was also noted that the floor was 'slight and rudely put together', while the front gable, with the top few courses of brickwork bedded on the incline, was 'very bad'.[39]

In more recent times, such chapels have continued to be despised: '...the starveling spires, the shoddy tracery and the hideous coloured glass of these mid-Victorian chapels came to be derided more bitterly than the solid Georgian classical chapels or the squat and homely "Little Bethels" ever had been; for the "Gothic" examples are manifestly pretentious, and snobbery is much more detestable than simplicity.'[40]

Nevertheless, however archaeologically incorrect, this was an enduring type of building and an expression of Victorian popular taste.

The conventional gallery – made of timber, with thin iron columns and a balcony front of panelling or ornamental ironwork, typically running along three sides of a rectangular chapel – was anathema to the Goth.' "Turn out the galleries" was a kind of battle cry with church restorers of the last generation,' wrote James Cubitt in 1892:

> And considering what sort of things galleries then were, both in churches and chapels, the cry was natural enough. The only question anybody ever asked about them was 'How many will they hold?' and the only way of beautifying them which anybody attempted was to put in a front filled with tawdry ornament and gilding. From this last fault, indeed, the chapel gallery was originally free. It was too baldly utilitarian to be meretricious. But its other faults were bad enough.[41]

Apart from problems of ventilation, acoustics, fire hazard and the awkward positions of some seats, the objection to these galleries was that they were mere fitments, not integral to the building, wholly lacking 'architectural' character.

Closely related to the matter of galleries was that of planning generally. In *Church Design for Congregations: Its Developments and Possibilities* (1870) Cubitt proposed solutions to these problems, putting them into practice a few years later in Union Chapel. He thought long rectangular plans unsuited to Nonconformist, particularly Congregationalist, needs. Everyone should be able to see and hear the service clearly. Cubitt argued for plans based on a large central area, accepting that galleries were essential if enough seats were to be provided within earshot of the preacher.

Centrally planned meeting-houses had been common in the 18th century. But partly because of Methodist influence, rectangular plans with the pulpit at one end on the long axis had become more usual. James Wilson of Bath proved adept at combining such plans with the Gothic style, winning a Methodist 'model chapel' competition.

Various experiments were made with central plans in the mid-19th century, including two Gothic-style chapels in Islington: Harecourt Chapel (1855) and Offord Road Chapel (1856–7). Both had modified Greek cross plans, as did Union Chapel. The important advance at Union Chapel was the full incorporation of the galleries into the structure of the building, contributing to instead of marring the architectural effect.

Central plans became popular with Congregationalists, but among Nonconformists generally there continued to be much overt copying of Anglican church architecture, with the nave-and-aisles plans, spires, ragstone facing and Decorated tracery common to so many Anglican churches. Camden Road New Church (1873) is typical.

Although Gothic predominated in Victorian chapel design, Romanesque and and occasionally Italianate styles were alternatives (e.g. Spencer Place Baptist Chapel, 1868–9, and Caledonian Road Primitive Methodist Chapel, 1870). Chapels continued to be built in the Classical style throughout the 19th century. Islington has a fine example, New Court Congregational Church (1870–1, now St Mellitus's Roman Catholic Church). Park Presbyterian Church, Grosvenor Avenue (1861–3, demolished), was unusually eclectic in style.

Roman Catholic churches

Until the passing of the Catholic Relief Act in 1791, the celebration of Mass was illegal in England except in the foreign Embassy chapels. These chapels subsequently acquired their own parishes, but other Roman Catholic parishes have arisen as missions, some of which originated in a handful of illegal Roman Catholic chapels. The earliest of these illegal chapels was Moorfields Chapel, City, founded in 1686, whose original parish included Islington, Finsbury, Clerkenwell, Hackney and Mile End. It was from Moorfields that a Roman Catholic mission was founded, in 1837, in Duncan Street. A parish church, St John the Evangelist, Duncan Terrace, was built in 1841–3.

Immigration, mostly from Ireland and Italy, produced a large Roman Catholic population in Islington and Clerkenwell from the 1840s onwards. 1846 saw the formation of an anti-Roman Catholic pressure group, the Islington Protestant Institute, and extremist Protestant feeling against Roman Catholics flared up sporadically into the 20th century.

The Irish were initially drawn to the area around the Angel and City Road, while the Italian community was concentrated in Clerkenwell and Holborn, in the Saffron Hill area. In and around Clerkenwell, the main religious centre for the Italians has long been St Peter's, Clerkenwell Road (built 1863), in the London Borough of Camden. St John the Evangelist has always been an important Irish centre.

Several Roman Catholic churches of architectural interest were built in the 19th and early 20th centuries throughout the present borough. St John the Evangelist, being Romanesque, was to Pugin's mind 'a temporary triumph to the infidels'.[42] Sacred Heart, Eden Grove (1869–70), is Gothic, but St Joseph's, Highgate Hill (1887–9, replacing a Gothic church of 1860–3 by E. W. Pugin) and Blessed Sacrament, Copenhagen Street (1916), were also Romanesque. The large convent of Notre Dame de Sion (1874–5) in Eden Grove, and the Passionists' Retreat at St Joseph's (1874–5) are both Italianate.

The 1960s saw the building of three Roman Catholic churches in Islington, two replacing long-standing temporary structures, one replacing a church in the London Borough of Hackney. St Joan of Arc (1961–2) was an attempt to combine Gothic form and planning with modernized detailing. St Gabriel's (1967–8) is an uncompromising, almost Brutalist design, with windowless walls and bare concrete; the plan resembles that of an 18th-century meeting-house.

Mission halls

By the late 19th century, the impetus for building new churches (other than those serving newly built-up districts) had weakened. All the main Nonconformist denominations were affected. There was instead an emphasis on the mission, with its aspirations to tackling social evils and providing social services. This was partly a reaction against the complacent view that if churches were built and good preachers booked congregations would grow automatically. It was also partly the result of the growing awareness of sections of the middle and upper classes of the dangerous inequities of urban society. The publication of *The Bitter Cry of Outcast London* in 1883 by the London Congregational Union was both symptomatic and influential in this regard.

The new mission halls often looked like any institutional, municipal or commercial buildings of the day. Increasingly, the place of worship itself was relegated, architecturally, to a subsidiary role. The London Domestic Mission in Dingley Place (1877), with its dour, warehouse-like façade, gives no outward sign of being a place of worship.

Many congregations founded missions in and around the neighbourhood and sometimes further afield. Union Chapel set up ragged schools in Bethnal Green and also took over a rusting 'tin tabernacle' near Highbury Station for local missionary work.

Exceptional circumstances produced one remarkable mission building: the Paget Memorial Mission Hall (1910–11).

Chapel-building between the wars

In the 1920s only two Nonconformist places of worship of significance were built in the present borough of Islington, both for existing congregations. The Seventh Day Adventist Church in Holloway Road (1927) was the first permanent home for a long-standing congregation and a national conference headquarters. The Methodist Central Hall in Drayton Park (1929–30) replaced two Victorian churches, one on the site, one in Liverpool Road.

This pattern continued in the 1930s. Bethany Hall in Barnsbury Road (1934) was built for an old-established Brethren group. Archway Central Methodist Hall (1933–4) was built on the site of a Victorian chapel. St Giles Christian Mission (1934–5) was an extensive remodelling of a Victorian chapel.

Post-war buildings

All or nearly all post-war Nonconformist churches in Islington replace buildings damaged by bombing, or given up since the war for a variety of reasons: structural failure, fire, dilapidation, excessive size, or unsuitability to present needs.

Cross Street Baptist Church and Highbury Quadrant Congregational Church are strongly conservative in design and reflect the austerity of the 1950s.

More progressive designs, from the late 1950s onwards, include Holloway United Reformed Church (1960) and Holly Park Methodist Church (1962). Unity Church (1958) is an example of the 'dual-purpose' church, for use as a church on Sundays and as a hall at other times. As a group, the post-war churches reflect the eclecticism and experimentation of post-war churches generally, occasionally tending towards pastiche or gimmickry but sometimes producing buildings of real quality such as Jewin Welsh Church (1960–1), the Roman Catholic Church of St Joan of Arc (1961–2) and St Gabriel's Roman Catholic Church (1966–8).

Architects

For many years, Nonconformist chapel-building nationally seemed to lag behind the architectural advance led by Anglicans and Roman Catholics. Partly this was a consequence of the sheer numbers of chapels built, their often small scale and shoe-string budgets. The development of the 'model chapel' system in the mid-19th century, whereby plans were supplied by 'mail order' or through publication, was a consequence of the huge demand for designs. But, taking no account of particular local circumstances, it only compounded matters, with debased designs cloned around the country.

Probably because of the number of architects competing for work in London, Islington largely escaped the model-chapel designers. This availability of architects was already marked by the early 19th century. The architects of few of the pre-Victorian chapels in Islington are known, but most were probably local or fairly local men. A. H. Hurst, architect of Pentonville Chapel, was a local resident. Northampton Tabernacle was by John Blyth, then of Goswell Road; Liverpool Road Wesleyan Chapel was by John Parkinson, architect and surveyor of Rahere Street, Goswell Road. The Scottish Presbyterian church in Colebrooke Row (1834) was by an obscure architect and surveyor from Furnival's Inn, Richard Dixon.

The practice of employing local architects continued. Jasper Cowell, architect of Upper Holloway Baptist Chapel (1866), practised locally. So did James Wesley Reed, architect of chapels in Barnsbury and Upper Holloway. Cowell's work included at least one Nonconformist building much further afield: the premises of the East of England Nonconformist School Company at Bishop's Stortford, Hertfordshire.

The main reason for this was that few Nonconformist chapels were designed in competition, open or limited. Holloway Congregational Chapel (1846) was – but since the chosen design was the work of one of the selectors it might just as well not have been.

It was not uncommon for architects to design chapels for churches of which they were members or with which they had some connection. Hurst was one of the original subscribers to Pentonville Chapel. Other examples include Cross Street Baptist Chapel (1852) by John Barnett, and New Court Congregational Church (1870–1) by Charles Searle. Sir Edwin Lutyens designed an apse for the church where his wife worshipped (c1926–30, at St Mary's Liberal Catholic Church, Caledonian Road). In some such cases, architects probably worked in an honorary capacity; George Lethbridge, architect of the Presbyterian mission hall, Elthorne Road (1907), and Ernest Trobridge, architect of ancillary buildings (1908) at Camden Road New Church, certainly did.

If not themselves local, architects were sometimes involved in other local work. Providence Baptist Chapel (1887), for example, is by C. J. Bentley, whose offices were in the City but who had recently built houses near the chapel on the Highbury Barn Estate.

There were architects who specialized in buildings for particular denominations. J. & J. Belcher, for example, designed a number of Catholic Apostolic churches in London and elsewhere, including one in Holloway (1873, now the Roman Catholic Church of SS Joseph and Padarn).

Provincial architects of Nonconformist chapels in Islington include J. McLansborough of Otley, West Yorkshire (Packington Street Methodist Chapel, 1854), W. F. Poulton, of the firm Poulton & Woodman, of Reading (Junction Road Congregational Church, 1866) and the ubiquitous Methodist, James Wilson of Bath. Bradshaw & Gass, of Bolton, won a competition to design the Leysian Mission, City Road (1903–4).

Buildings by famous architects are few. George Dance the Younger's role in the design of Wesley's Chapel (1777–8) remains uncertain, but in any case the circumstances were unusual. Among the better-known names are James Cubitt (Union Chapel, 1876–7), T. E. Knightley (Trinity Presbyterian Church, 1858), and A. Beresford Pite (Paget Memorial Mission Hall, 1910–11).

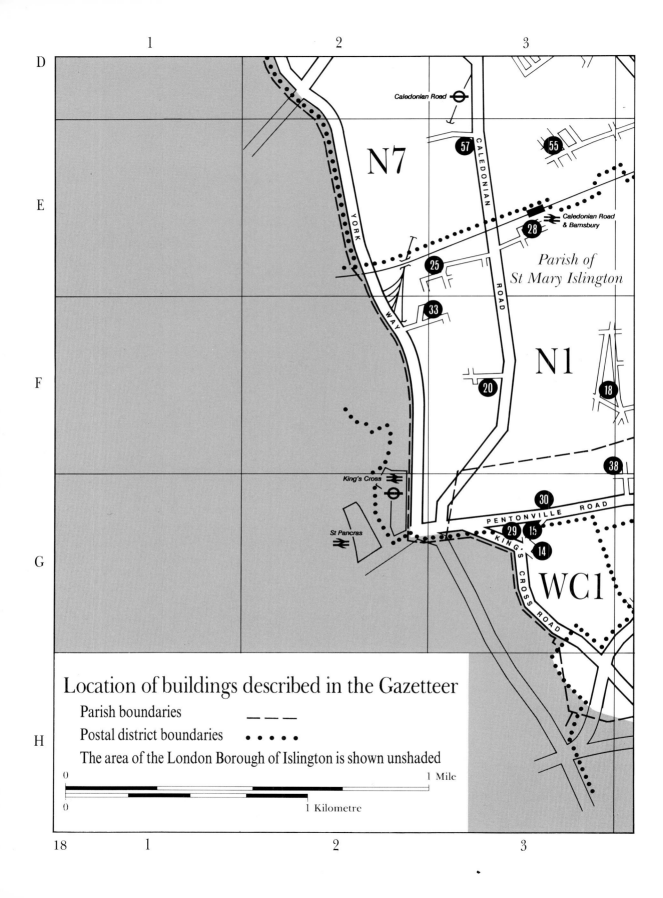

Location of buildings described in the Gazetteer

Parish boundaries — — —

Postal district boundaries • • • • •

The area of the London Borough of Islington is shown unshaded

0   1 Mile

0   1 Kilometre

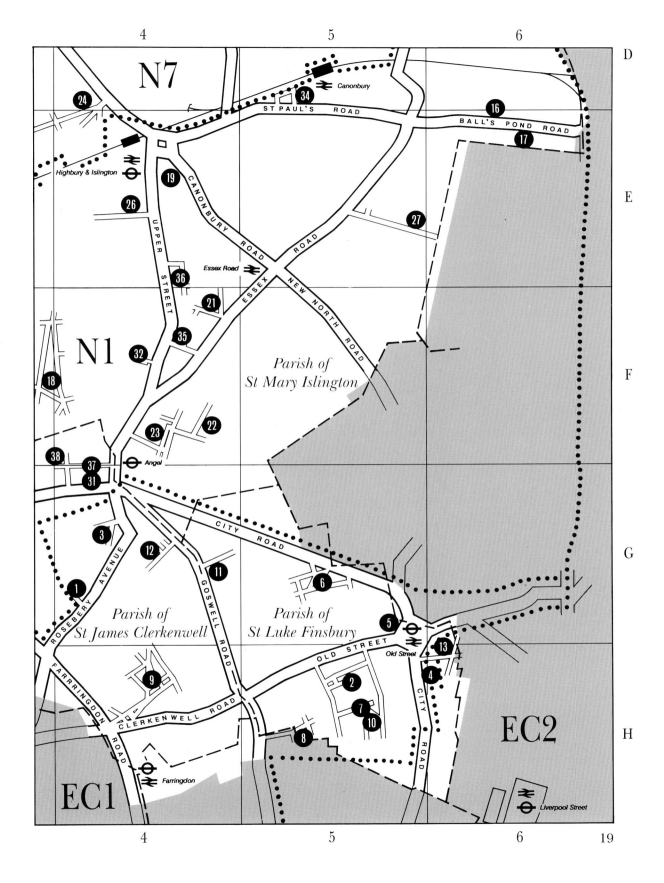

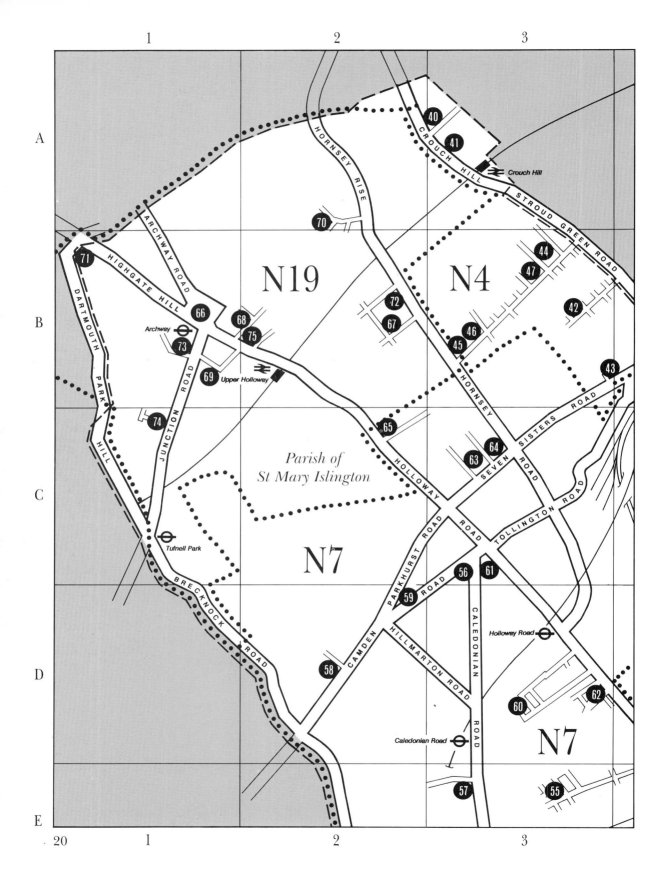

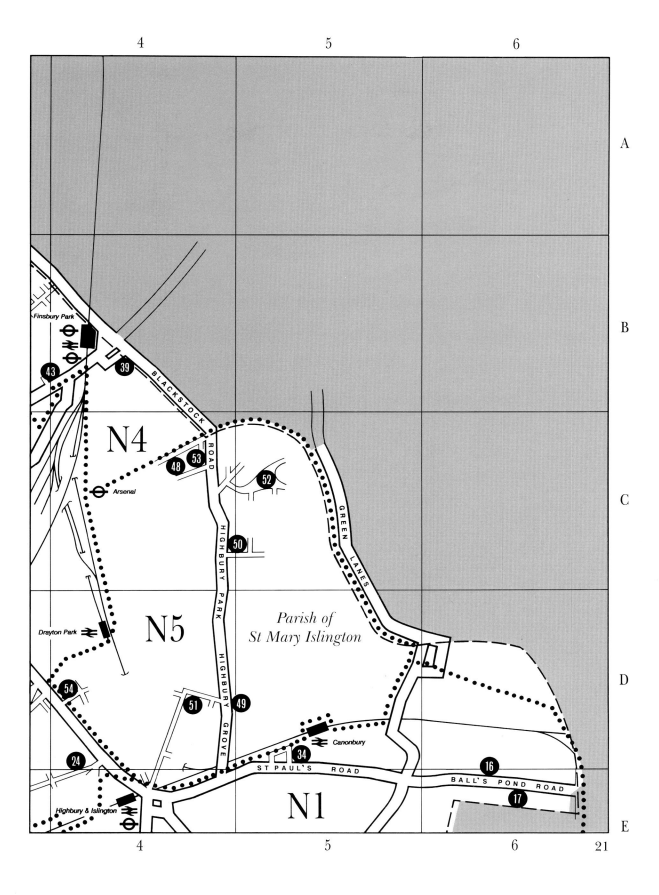

Key to Map

EC1

1   Roman Catholic Church of SS Peter and Paul, Amwell Street **4G**
2   Bunhill Fields Meeting House, Banner Street **5H**
3   Angel Baptist Church, Chadwell Street **4G**
4   Wesley's Chapel, City Road **6H**
5   Former Leysian Mission, City Road **5G**
6   Former London Domestic Mission, Dingley Place **5G**
7   Former Leysian Mission, Errol Street **5H**
8   Jewin Welsh Church, Fann Street **5H**
9   Woodbridge Chapel, Hayward's Place **4H**
10 St Joseph's Roman Catholic Church, Lamb's Buildings **5H**
11 Finsbury Mission, Moreland Street **4G**
12 Former Independent chapel, Rawstorne Street **4G**

EC2

13 Former Whitefield Tabernacle, Leonard Street **6H**

WC1

14 Vernon Baptist Chapel, King's Cross Road **3G**
15 Former Claremont Chapel District School, King's Cross Road **3G**

N1

16 Roman Catholic Church of Our Lady and St Joseph, Ball's Pond Road **6E**
17 Former Maberly Chapel, Ball's Pond Road **6E**
18 Former Bethany Hall, Barnsbury Road **3F**
19 Union Chapel, Compton Terrace **4E**
20 Blessed Sacrament Roman Catholic Church, Copenhagen Street **3F**
21 Cross Street Baptist Church **4F**
22 Roman Catholic Church of Our Lady of Czestochowa and St Casimir, Devonia Road **4F**

23 Roman Catholic Church of St John the Evangelist, Duncan Terrace **4F**
24 Former Sandemanian meeting-house, Furlong Road **4D**
25 Former Gifford Hall, Gifford Street **3E**
26 Christian meeting-room, Islington Park Street **4E**
27 Former manse, Trinity Presbyterian Church, Northchurch Road **5E**
28 Former Congregational chapel, Offord Road **3E**
29 King's Cross Welsh Tabernacle, Pentonville Road **3G**
30 Grimaldi Park House, Pentonville Road **3G**
31 Former Claremont Chapel, Pentonville Road **4G**
32 Former Providence Chapel, Providence Place **4F**
33 Paget Memorial Mission Hall, Randell's Road **3F**
34 Harecourt United Reformed Church, St Paul's Road **5D**
35 Former Islington Chapel, Upper Street **4F**
36 Unity Church, Upper Street **4E**
37 Islington Claremont United Reformed Church, White Lion Street **4G**
38 First Born Church of the Living God, White Lion Street **4F**

N4

39 Christadelphian hall, Blackstock Road **4B**
40 Former Fifth Church of Christ Scientist, Blythwood Road **3A**
41 Holly Park Methodist Church, Crouch Hill **3A**
42 Former Congregational mission hall, Lennox Road **3B**
43 Former Sunday school, Finsbury Park Congregational Church, Playford Road **3B**
44 Newcourt Centre (Elim Pentecostal Church), Regina Road **3B**
45 Zoar Hall, Tollington Park **3B**
46 Tollington Park Baptist Chapel **3B**
47 St Mellitus's Roman Catholic Church, Tollington Park **3B**

N5

48 Former Wesleyan Methodist chapel, Gillespie Road **4C**

49 Former Highbury Grove Chapel **4D**
50 Roman Catholic Church of St Joan of Arc, Highbury Park **4C**
51 Providence Baptist Chapel, Highbury Place **4D**
52 Highbury Quadrant Congregational Church **5C**
53 Former Congregational mission hall, Hurlock Street **4C**
54 Citadel Buildings, Ronalds Road **4D**

N7

55 St Giles Christian Mission, Bride Street **3E**
56 Holloway United Reformed Church, Caledonian Road **3C**
57 Caledonian Road Methodist Church **3E**
58 Camden Road Baptist Church **2D**
59 Former Camden Road New Church **2D**
60 Sacred Heart of Jesus Roman Catholic Church, Eden Grove **3D**
61 Holloway Seventh Day Adventist Church, Holloway Road **3C**
62 Islington Central Methodist Church, Palmer Place **3D**
63 Roman Catholic Church of SS Joseph and Padarn, Salterton Road **3C**
64 Holloway Welsh Chapel, Sussex Way **3C**
65 Upper Holloway Baptist Church, Tollington Way **2C**

N19

66 Archway Central Hall, Archway Close **1B**
67 Former Congregational mission hall, Bavaria Road **2B**
68 Former Presbyterian mission hall, Elthorne Road **2B**
69 Hargrave Hall, Hargrave Road **1B**
70 Hornsey Rise Baptist Chapel, Hazellville Road **2A**
71 St Joseph's Roman Catholic Church, Highgate Hill **1B**
72 North London Spiritualist Church, Hornsey Road **2B**
73 Archway Citadel, Junction Road **1B**
74 Former Junction Road Congregational Church **1C**
75 St Gabriel's Roman Catholic Church, St John's Villas **2B**

Gazetteer

EC1

1   Roman Catholic Church of SS Peter and Paul

Amwell (formerly Rosoman) Street EC1   Grade II listed
(formerly Northampton Tabernacle)

Northampton Tabernacle was built in 1835, on a lease from the Marquis of Northampton, by members of the Countess of Huntingdon's Connexion who had seceded from Spa Fields Chapel. After some years of bickering between minister and congregation, it closed. The lease was sold off by the Court of Chancery in 1847 to a Catholic mission, set up in 1842 by two Spanish priests in part of a disused workhouse in Saffron Hill.

The architect of Northampton Tabernacle was John Blyth, a surveyor practising in Goswell Road. It is Italianate in style, with a symmetrical stuccoed façade in three bays containing a large Venetian window over the entrance.

It is oblong in plan, with a gallery, supported on iron columns and balustraded with Gothic-style cast-iron panels, running over

Roman Catholic Church of SS Peter and Paul in 1990

Roman Catholic Church of SS Peter and Paul in 1990

the entrance vestibule and most of the way along the sides. The ceiling is coffered. A blind arch carried on Corinthian pilasters decorates the sanctuary wall; the sanctuary itself has recently been remodelled, the Gothic-style altar rails having been removed and new light oak furniture, by Ormsby of Scarisbrick, installed.

Four stained glass windows, all of post-war date, depict SS Anthony of Padua, Vincent Pallotti, Thérèse of Lisieux and Martin de Porres respectively.

At the rear of the church is a school, rebuilt in 1877 and subsequently enlarged.

2   Bunhill Fields Meeting House

Banner Street EC1
(Memorial Buildings)

The meeting-house stands in the Quaker burial ground, purchased by the Friends in 1661 and later enlarged, which was closed by Order in Council in 1855. Meetings were held in a tent in the graveyard in 1874, and a permanent mission was projected two years later.

Funds became available in 1880 through the purchase by the Metropolitan Board of Works of part of the ground for road-widening. The result was Bunhill Fields Memorial Buildings, built in 1881 and extended in 1888. A substantial complex in the Queen Anne style, it comprised a mission hall, schools and coffee tavern. The architect was William Ward Lee, Surveyor to the Society of Friends. The builder was William Brass of Old Street.

The present meeting-house is all that remains of the Memorial Buildings, of which it formed a wing. The rest was destroyed by bombing in the Second World War.

The graveyard is now maintained as a public park. Among the 12,000 or so Quakers buried here is George Fox (1624–90), founder of the movement. Two gravestones, a 19th-century headstone and a modern replacement, record the fact. A stone, salvaged from the wreckage and now kept at the meeting-house, records the dedication of the Memorial Buildings to Fox and the Quaker martyrs and the furtherance of religious, moral and philanthropic objects.

3   Angel Baptist Church

Chadwell Street EC1   Grade II listed
(formerly Mount Zion Chapel)

Angel Baptist Church was built as Providence Chapel for a congregation of Calvinistic Methodists. The promoter was Thomas Elliott, Esq, of Claremont Terrace, Pentonville, who agreed to lease the site from the New River Company in 1821. By July 1823 nothing had been done with the ground and Elliott had to explain himself at a New River Company board meeting, promising 'to begin the work on Tuesday morning next, and to proceed thence forward with due diligence'.[1]

The chapel was completed by April 1824, together with a small house at the rear, which Elliott had built, contrary to the original

Angel Baptist Church in 1991

agreement. The houses on either side of the chapel, with which it forms part of a terrace, were built at the same time by a Mr Hall.

In 1827 the congregation left, probably moving on to a new chapel in Rawstorne Street (Gazetteer **12**) with which Elliott was involved, and the building was taken over by disgruntled former members of the Scottish Presbyterian church in Regent Square (now demolished). This congregation left after a few years, building a chapel in Colebrooke Row (*see* Notes on Demolished Buildings). In 1853, after further congregations had come and gone (one of them to Rawstorne Street Chapel, then a school), it was acquired by the present Strict Baptist congregation and renamed Mount Zion Chapel. Recently the more local name has been adopted.

It is a small Classical-style building, stucco-fronted, with round-arched windows and a tetrastyle Ionic portico (the capitals of the outer columns now lacking volutes). [2] The front is in four bays, the central bays brought slightly forward and rising to a pediment flanked by vases.

Inside, part of a Classical treatment survives, notably in the ornamentation of the wall behind the pulpit and the doorways leading to the vestry behind. The ceiling was removed in 1873, the trusses stained and the roof matchboarded. The Gothic-style pitch-pine pews are also Victorian. The pulpit, now much shortened, was originally entered up stairs from the vestry.

The baptistery, concealed beneath the floor, was installed in 1855.

At the rear of the chapel, the house was demolished and a school built in 1929–30. Solid and well built in a simple neo-Georgian style, it was designed by Herbert A. Wright of Pentonville Road. It was built in addition to a Sunday school opened in 1897 in White Lion Street, Pentonville (Gazetteer **38**).

4   Wesley's Chapel

City Road EC1   Grade I listed

Wesley's Chapel and the original buildings in the 'chapel square' were built as part of the smart residential development of Finsbury overseen by George Dance the Younger, Surveyor to the City of London Corporation. The City had held the land, a prebendal estate of St Paul's Cathedral, on lease for centuries.

Wesley mentioned the project to replace his old headquarters, the Foundery (*see* Introduction), in a letter to his brother Charles in March 1775. The design was settled in November 1776 and the contract was taken up by Samuel Tooth, a local builder and timber merchant. Tooth, a former preacher, was a friend of the Wesley family. The foundation stone was laid on 21 April 1777 and on 1 November 1778 the 'New Chapel' opened.

The 1776 building lease, for sixty-one years, specified the erection of a terrace of five first-rate houses fronting City Road with a central carriage-entrance to the chapel behind. The buildings should have been up within four years, but by March 1779 the houses had not been started. Wesley successfully petitioned for a simpler design, getting a new lease stipulating that the houses should conform to revised elevations by Dance.

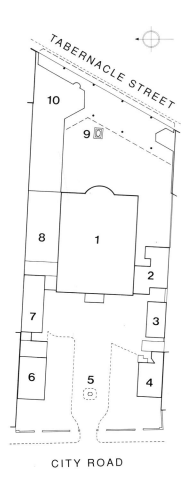

1   Chapel
2   Foundery Chapel
3   Chapel-keeper's house
4   Wesley's House
5   Statue of Wesley
6   Manse
7   Benson Building
8   Radnor Hall
9   Wesley's tomb
10 Modern office development

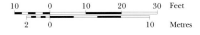

Block plan of Wesley's Chapel and ancillary buildings. Based on a plan by Trevor Wilkinson Associates, architects (1979), and additional measurements taken 1991

Wesley moved in to the first house that August. Nearly five years later, the others were still unbuilt. He obtained permission to build only one more and to rail the rest of the frontage, with gates to 'leave a handsome opening to the Chapel'.[3] The second house was subsequently built, together with two smaller houses facing each other across the chapel square.

There is uncertainty as to who was responsible for the design of the chapel. Dance has been suggested as the architect; his assistant James Peacock may have had a hand in the work. Wesley's comment on the deliberations of the building committee is vague and ambiguous: 'We considered the several plans which were offered for the new chapel. Having agreed upon one, we desired a surveyor to draw out the particulars...'[4]

Even if preliminary drawings were prepared by Dance or Peacock, it is likely that another architect produced the final designs – such as Mr Carr, probably James Carr (c1742–1821), who was employed to survey and value the houses belonging to the chapel in 1793; or Thomas Leverton (1743–1824), who exhibited a design for a chapel 'now building' in 1777.[5]

The original character of Wesley's Chapel has been submerged by the embellishments of successive improvers, restorers, and memorializers in stained glass and stone. Various alterations were made inside and out in the early 19th century. Some if not most of these were overseen by the Revd William Jenkins, an architect who was a supernumerary minister on the London circuit in 1806–10. Jenkins' work certainly included the renovation of the roof, during which 'nearly as much timber was cut out...as would suffice to support another roof nearly as large'.[6]

Finsbury's decline as a residential district in the 19th century may well have helped to preserve the chapel. Falling takings from pew-rents undermined the finances, and there was no incentive to enlarge or rebuild on a grander scale. In 1860 the architect W. W. Pocock warned that the City Road houses might have to be let as shops: 'the locality has changed its character so much that...much difficulty is experienced in inducing Ministers to occupy these houses as residences...'[7]

It did not come to that, and the reversion of the Finsbury Estate from the City to the Church Commissioners made possible the purchase of the freehold in 1862, following which Pocock supervised the first of several restorations of the chapel. Changes made at this time included re-pewing, extending the seating area up to the entrance (this end of the chapel had always been left open, for latecomers to stand), the making of separate entrances to the gallery, and the lowering of the pulpit by several feet.

After a serious fire in 1879 an apparently meticulous restoration was carried out, the architect being Charles Bell and the builder J. D. Hobson of Adelphi. It was reported at the time that 'all the old and familiar features have been reproduced'.[8] These included the ceiling, replicated from fragments, and one of the pillars supporting the sanctuary arch.

The restoration carried out in 1891 by the architect Elijah Hoole and the contractors Holloway Brothers, to mark the centenary of Wesley's death, was far more extensive and did much to alter the original character of the building. It involved the laying of new concrete foundations[9] and the reconstruction of much of the brickwork. The ceiling was raised four feet to make room for tiered seating on the gallery, which had originally been flat. The wooden columns[10] supporting the gallery were replaced with columns of jasper and relegated to the new vestibule. Mosaic floors were laid. The seating was again renewed, nearly all the work being done by country firms because of a strike by the London carpenters and joiners. A new organ (replacing one installed in 1882 at the West end) was fitted, with the pipes in the side galleries and the console in front of the choir stalls. An idea of Hoole's, which was not implemented, was to decorate the cove of the ceiling with festooned tablets commemorating Methodist worthies. Outside, the forecourt railings were replaced and John Wesley's statue erected.

Further extensive renovation had to be carried out in the 1920s. In 1938 the organ was reconstructed and moved to its present position at the West end.

In 1972 another crisis of dilapidation was reached. Restoration, by Trevor Wilkinson Associates, architects, was funded through a worldwide appeal. Completed in 1979, it was low key compared to the 1891 restoration, the most obvious change being the replacement of the vestibule screen.

The front of the chapel is in five bays, the middle bays pedimented, with a central doorway and round-arched windows on two levels.

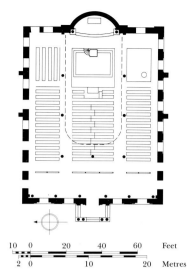

Wesley's Chapel. Based on a plan by Trevor Wilkinson Associates, architects (1979)

Wesley's Chapel. View from John Wesley's bedroom, Wesley's House, in 1990

This arrangement is original, as is the fluted frieze beneath the pediment, but some features are later. The portico was added *c*1815. Other additions, including the first-floor window surrounds and the rusticated quoins, date from 1891.

The interior, oblong in plan with an apsidal sanctuary, is galleried on three sides. Decoratively, the chief features of interest are the ceiling and the sanctuary. Both incorporate the Vitruvian scroll pattern which forms (in Coade stone) the frieze on the front of Wesley's House. The ceiling is in the Adam style, mainly geometrical, with partly gilded enrichments including cherubim. The polished granite pillars of the sanctuary arch, replacing piers painted to resemble marble, were installed in memory of the Revd Samuel Waddy (1804–76).

There are few furnishings of individual note, the main item being Wesley's pulpit. The font, installed in 1891 with a new pedestal and top, is medieval.

The first stained glass was set in the apse in the 1880s, and in 1891 a scheme for the whole chapel, illustrating the origins and progress of Methodism, was projected. But the plan foundered, and instead various windows were installed from time to time until

(This page)
Wesley's Chapel. Monuments by John Adams-Acton (left) and E. Onslow Ford

(Opposite)
Wesley's Chapel in 1990

1934. They include works by Henry Holiday, Mayer & Co. of Munich, James Powell of Whitefriars, and Frank O. Salisbury.

There are many mural tablets. The sculptors of the earlier works include James Bubb, Nevil Northey Burnard, John Bacon & Samuel Manning, John Cusworth and Thomas Porter. Late 19th-century monuments include several busts, some by John Adams-Acton and a pair, under Gothic canopies, by E. Onslow Ford.

Adams-Acton also sculpted the bronze statue of Wesley in the forecourt, about the clay model for which he wrote in late 1891: 'My whole time is given to this statue and everything is subservient to it and I shall daily be working with soul and energy until it is quite finished...'[11]

The Foundery Chapel, originally called the Morning Chapel, was enlarged in 1864, gutted in the 1879 fire and rebuilt in 1899. It contains seating from the Foundery and a chamber organ which belonged to Charles Wesley.

Wesley's House (No. 47 City Road) was restored as a Wesley memorial and museum in 1897–8. It is now augmented by the Museum of Methodism in the crypt beneath the chapel, opened in 1984, where exhibits include the pulpit from the Foundery.

Wesley's Chapel. Seating installed 1891, showing extendable ends

The graveyard, Wesley's Chapel, in 1990. John Wesley's tomb is in the foreground

The other City Road house (No. 49) was replaced by the present manse in 1880. The Benson Building at the side of the manse was built about the same time, to provide a church parlour, library, reading- and meeting-rooms. It commemorates the Revd Joseph Benson (1749–1821), one of the great Methodist preachers. On the other side of the yard is the house, now the chapel-keeper's house, where Benson wrote his *Notes, Critical, Explanatory, and Practical* on the Bible and where he died.

The graveyard behind the chapel, its character uncomfortably altered in recent years by the erection of a mirror-finish office building on two sides, contains Wesley's tomb. When the vault was left open for another interment years later, thieves stole lead from his coffin and in 1828 the body was reinterred and the vault sealed. The graveyard was closed by Order in Council in 1853.

5   Former Leysian Mission

City Road EC1   Grade II listed

The third home of the Methodist mission founded in 1886 by old boys of the Leys School, Cambridge, this is one of the most ambitious buildings of its kind. Designed in competition by the Bolton architects Bradshaw & Gass and built by Holliday & Greenwood, it was completed in 1904 and opened by the Prince and Princess of Wales.

The façade might be that of a town hall or a commercial office block. Symmetrical and repetitious, the front is of terracotta, ornamented in Arts and Crafts motifs, with red granite facings on the ground floor. With shallow oriel windows and slight projection to the central bays, it has a looming, cliff-like presence, relieved by a large copper-domed cupola.

Commercial premises in the form of offices and shops occupy part of the front, but the bulk of the building was designed to accommodate the innumerable functions of the mission: 'clubs...for working men, young women, members of the Boys' Brigade, and Sunday School girls and boys; prayer meetings, services, and old-fashioned Methodist class-meetings and Sunday-schools...medical mission, thrift clubs, gymnasium and drill classes for lads and girls, a poor man's lawyer, athletic clubs, lectures and entertainments, guilds of play for the children, a labour bureau...'[12]

Former Leysian Mission, City Road. Detail of terracotta work

Underlying the work of the mission was the idea of the missionary hostel or 'settlement'. Two settlements offered long- or short-term accommodation to Old Leysians taking part in missionary work, or simply needing somewhere to stay in London; another housed a team of sisters and 'lady-workers'.

At the heart of the mission was the Great Hall, a galleried church-cum-concert hall seating 1,750. A Lesser Hall held 600. Bombing in the Second World War wrecked the Great Hall and other parts of the building. In 1953–5 the Great Hall was rebuilt to the designs of W. H. Gunton. Opened by H.M. the Queen Mother, the new hall has a shallow barrel-vaulted ceiling. Behind the platform, a panel of small bricks as a background to a plain cross, with fluted stone piers on each side, constitute almost the only ornamentation. The hall was fitted with the simplest tubular steel tip-up seating. There is no gallery; the tiers of the old hall still exist, walled off at the rear.

(Opposite)
Former Leysian Mission, City Road. View from Old Street roundabout in 1991

With the exception of the central staircase, faced in marble, and spacious landings, little of architectural interest survives internally. Since the amalgamation of the mission with Wesley's Chapel, in March 1989, the building has been largely empty, awaiting redevelopment or conversion to new uses.

6 Former London Domestic Mission

Dingley (formerly George's) Place EC1

The London Domestic Mission Society, a Unitarian venture, was founded in 1835. The mission in Dingley Place was built in 1877. Plain and functional, in the simplified Queen Anne style used for many low-cost commercial and institutional premises, it comprised a schoolroom and hall above, together with a wing containing living accommodation and a games room. The architect was Thomas Chatfeild Clarke.

The building is now owned by the London Borough of Islington and is used as an 'intermediate treatment' centre for young persons in care.

7 Former Leysian Mission

No. 12 Errol Street EC1

Built in 1889–90 to replace the mission's original premises in Whitecross Street, No. 12 Errol Street was designed by W. H. Boney, an Old Leysian, and built by Holloway Brothers. Soon outgrown, it was replaced in 1904 by the Leysian Mission in City Road (Gazetteer 5). Subsequently in commercial use, it is now occupied by the Arts Educational Schools' Drama Department.

In the Queen Anne style, it has a gabled front crowned by the arms of the Leys School in cut and rubbed brick. A large bulls-eye window lights a gallery overlooking the main hall or chapel. Decorative cartouches either side of the entrance have been removed.

8 Jewin Welsh Church

Fann Street EC1
(Welsh Presbyterian)

The origins of the church go back to 1774, when a Welsh Calvinistic Methodist congregation was founded in Smithfield, moving from there to Wilderness Row and later Jewin Crescent. The name Jewin was retained when a new chapel was built on the present site in 1878–9. This was severely damaged by bombing in 1940 (*see* Notes on Demolished Buildings).

After the war, plans for a new church in Snow Hill had to be given up when the site was designated for office development. However, the sale of the ground gave ample funds for rebuilding at Fann Street. The new church, designed by Caroe & Partners, was built by F. & M. F. Higgs Ltd. in 1960–1.

(Opposite)
Jewin Welsh Church in 1990

It is rectangular in plan, brick built with a pitched copper-covered roof. The square West tower has a pyramidal roof with a distinctive, rather baroque finial. Inside, a gallery with tiered seating on three sides continues as an organ gallery at the East end.

The interior finish is of a high standard, the woodwork of unpolished smoked American oak being a particularly attractive feature. The West window, triangular headed with mullions and diagonal tracery, contains stained glass by Carl Edwards depicting the dissemination of the Word of God and images of the London Blitz. Edwards also designed the memorial clerestory window to the Revd D. S. Owens (d. 1959).

Attached to the church are a large hall with a stage and green-room, vestries and caretaker's residence.

9 Woodbridge Chapel

Hayward's Place EC1   Grade II listed

The site is part of the former country estate of Thomas Sekforde, Master of the Court of Requests to Queen Elizabeth, which he left on trust for the support of almshouses in his home town of Woodbridge in Suffolk. The estate was mostly built up in the late 18th century, but was extensively redeveloped in 1827–8.

Woodbridge Chapel, built in 1832–3 for Independent High Calvinists, follows the simple Classical style of the neighbouring streets and is built in the same yellow brick, with stucco dressings.

Internally, little of the original treatment survives, with the exception of blind arcading on the wall at the back of the pulpit. Most of the present fittings and furnishings, including the gallery and seating, are Victorian.

In 1894 the chapel was taken over by John Alfred Groom (1845–1919) for the Watercress and Flower Girls' Christian Mission which he founded in 1866. It was for many years the

Woodbridge Chapel in 1990

Woodbridge Chapel. Disused 19th-century organ on West gallery

Woodbridge Chapel in 1990

centre of Groom's mission, which provided social support for street flower sellers (including accommodation in houses nearby, known as the Crippleage) and industrial training for blind and crippled girls. The basement of the chapel, considerably deepened, was used by the mission as a paper-flower factory. Groom is commemorated by a small oak memorial in the chapel.

Shortly before the end of the Second World War, John Groom's Association for the Disabled (as the mission became [13]) let the premises to the Islington Medical Mission, one of a number of missions founded by the Medical Missionary Association in the latter 19th century. The mission was then operating temporarily at Islington Chapel, Upper Street (Gazetteer **35**), having been bombed out of its home in Britannia Row, a Congregational mission chapel (*see* Notes on Demolished Buildings).

The chapel is now owned by the Clerkenwell and Islington Medical Mission, which holds Sunday services and runs an NHS surgery in the former Sunday school adjoining.

10 St Joseph's Roman Catholic Church

Lamb's Buildings EC1

The church forms part of the former St Joseph's Schools (now occupied as commercial premises, partly by the *Catholic Herald*), built in 1901 to replace a church and schools erected on the same site in 1856. There had been an orphanage and schools here since 1815, when the ground was purchased by Catholic charities. St Joseph's Church originated in 1848 as a mission from St Mary, Moorfields, and was from 1901 to 1922 a chapel of ease to St Mary's.

Its predecessor was built over the schools; the present church is in the basement. A rectangular room, it is lit by large round-arched windows, three of which contain stained glass. One, depicting the Agony in the Garden, is the survivor of a set of three from St Mary, Moorfields.[14] The others illustrated the death of St Joseph and the Descent from the Cross.

Furnishings include several statues said also to have come from Moorfields, and an urn-like oval font. The Stations of the Cross are modern reliefs; an old set which came from the Convent of Mercy in Crispin Street, Spitalfields, is still kept at the church.

11 Finsbury Mission

Moreland (formerly Charles) Street EC1
(formerly Spencer Place Baptist Chapel)

Spencer Place Baptist Chapel was built in 1868–9, retaining the name of its predecessor in Spencer Place, Goswell Road (*see* Notes on Demolished Buildings). A Romanesque-style building comprising a rectangular nave with clerestory, galleries, corner tower with spire, and basement schoolrooms, it was built of stock brick with orange brick banding and stone dressings. It was designed by Finch Hill & Paraire and built by Hill & Sons.

The chapel eventually became an interdenominational Free Church mission, latterly a branch of the Shaftesbury Society. Rebuilding was envisaged in 1953, but gave way to extensive

Finsbury Mission in 1990

remodelling, completed in 1958, by W. H. Gunton, architect. The building was much reduced in height and remodelled internally. Since 1978 it has been the premises of RIBA Publications Ltd.

12 Former Independent chapel

No. 48 Rawstorne Street EC1

A plain brick building with stucco dressings, Rawstorne Street Chapel looks much like a small warehouse, an impression reinforced by a loading-door inserted on the first floor. It was built in 1828 by Independents, including Thomas Boucher, hosier, of Middle Row, Holborn, on a seventy-year building lease.

The site, part of Hermitage Fields, once owned by the Knights Hospitaller, has an earlier history of use by Nonconformists. Part of the Dame Alice Owen Estate, belonging to a charitable trust set up in 1613 and administered by the Brewers' Company, some five acres of Hermitage Fields were partly developed by Thomas Rawstorne, a builder, from 1773 to 1781. When Rawstorne went bankrupt, a large area, including the site of the chapel, was leased by the Society of Friends, who built a school and workhouse in 1786. The Quakers moved to Croydon in 1825, and in 1827 pulled down the old school and began selling off the land on long building leases.

The chapel had a short life as a place of worship. In 1837 it was up for sale, complete with pulpit, pews and reading-desk, but with manufacturing a suggested alternative use. In 1855 it was converted to a National School, by William Slater, architect, which it remained until c1890. After a brief spell in the occupation of the Salvation Army at the turn of the century, it was used for a succession of commercial and industrial purposes. It was for many years a printing works, and is now a clothing factory.

An extension at the back, originally the vestry, has been rebuilt.

Former Independent chapel, No. 48 Rawstorne Street, in 1990

EC2

13 Former Whitefield Tabernacle

Leonard Street EC2

Built in 1868 to replace the Tabernacle erected for George Whitefield in 1752–3 (*see* Introduction and Notes on Demolished Buildings), this former Congregational church is now occupied by the Central Foundation School for Boys, after many years in commercial use. Not long after the rebuilding, the congregation began to decline, as members moved to the suburbs and local residential streets were redeveloped with factories and warehouses. Blackened with grime, by 1909 it had acquired 'an antiquated appearance rather out of keeping with its age'.[1] Ministerless since 1920, it was not finally closed until 1958.

Gothic-style, faced in Kentish Rag coursed rubble with Portland and Bath stone dressings, it was designed by C. G. Searle & Son and built by Dove Brothers. The Leonard Street façade is a boldly designed gable front containing a triple pointed window with Geometrical tracery. There are three linked arched doorways, the arches carried on short shafts of blue Bristol stone with stiff-leaf capitals. At the side is the former Sunday school, similar in style.

Both buildings have had a first floor inserted. The timber roof trusses, of some elaboration, remain exposed. The upper floors are used respectively for games and art classes.

Former Whitefield Tabernacle in 1990

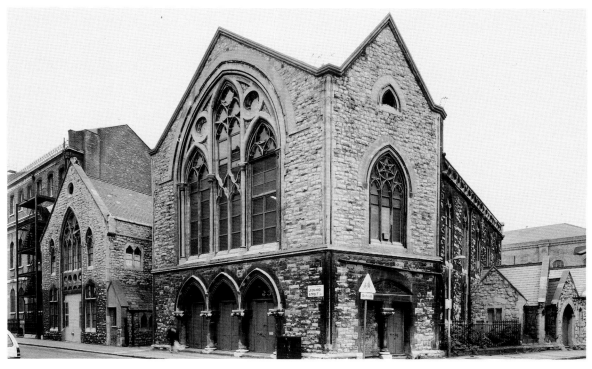

WC1

14 Vernon Baptist Chapel

King's Cross Road WC1

Vernon Chapel was built in 1843–4 by the Revd Owen Clarke (*c*1791–1859), secretary of the British and Foreign Temperance Society, on a seventy-five-year lease from the New River Company. Clarke also took a house plot on either side of the chapel, giving him the whole of the principal side of Vernon Square. 'The Chapel,' he wrote, 'will be Gothic but so disposed as to harmonize as far as practicable with the buildings near it.' [1]

The houses built by Clarke were three storeys high with basements, brick built with rusticated stuccoed ground-floor fronts. One was replaced in 1933 by Vernon Hall, the other (bombed in 1941) by the present manse, built in 1962 (Edmund E. Swaine, architect).

Brick built, with stone dressings, the chapel had a gabled front in three bays with buttresses and tall pinnacles, the outer bays carried up to a horizontal cornice following the line of the parapets of the houses. The façade still stands, somewhat altered. The basement of the chapel was used as a school.

Vernon Baptist Chapel in 1990

The designer of the buildings is not known, but it is probable that Clarke was acting as his own architect, in conjunction with the builder, William Smith of White Lion Street, Pentonville.

After Clarke's death, his trustees evicted the congregation for non-payment of rent and leased the chapel to a minister from Spencer Place Baptist Chapel. It has remained the home of the same congregation ever since.

In about 1848 galleries were added and in 1869–70 the chapel was enlarged by John Goodchild, architect, a member of the congregation. The nave was extended over the site of vestries at the East end, and short transepts added. Extensive reconstruction was carried out following structural failure in 1937. The walls were lowered by several feet and the interior was completely remodelled. Sawday Hall, behind the manse, was built at this time.

The chapel was badly damaged by land mines in 1941, reopening in 1951. It is oblong in plan, with canted corners at the East end and an alcove between, containing the organ, and has a shallow barrel-vaulted ceiling.

15 Former Claremont Chapel District School

King's Cross Road WC1

In 1847 a small Sunday school was built in connection with Claremont Chapel (Gazetteer 31), in a former mason's yard off Bagnigge Wells Road (now King's Cross Road), west of what is now Lorenzo Street. An oblong hall with a simple arched brace roof, it was designed by John Tarring and built for about £320; the tucked away site gave no scope for architectural display. It is now in commercial use.

N1

16 Roman Catholic Church of Our Lady and St Joseph

Ball's Pond Road N1

The church, presbytery and church hall were built in 1964 to replace a church south of Ball's Pond Road in Hackney. The architect was Wilfred C. Mangan of Preston, Lancashire, a designer of Roman Catholic churches since the 1920s. The complex is spaciously planned, plain in style, built of yellow brick with pitched copper-covered roofs.

The West front of the church, facing the street, has three round-arched entrances, the tympanum of the middle doorway containing a relief carving of Our Lady, St Joseph and the Infant Jesus. The central bay, brought slightly forward, rises to a tower.

The church comprises an oblong nave with a curved ceiling and a narrower sanctuary flanked by a sacristy and a Lady Chapel.

17 Former Maberly Chapel[1]

Ball's Pond Road N1   Grade II listed

This 'unpretending edifice' – as Thomas Cromwell described it in his *Walks through Islington* (1835) – was built as an Independent chapel in 1825 by Henry Ashley, on a sixty-one-year lease. Ashley also built the houses on either side. It is named after William Maberly, the ground landlord.

Maberly Chapel was the 'birthplace'[2] of the London City Mission, founded in 1835, one of many missions in Great Britain and overseas set up by David Nasmith (1799–1839), at that time a member of Union Chapel. Closed *c*1891, it was renamed Earlham Hall and used by the North East London Mission. The Earlham Institute for Working Girls was run at No. 55 nearby. In the 1920s it was a Brethren meeting-house before becoming a printing works. It remained in commercial use until its dereliction in recent years.

It is a stucco-fronted Classical-style building, of oblong plan. The front has two entrances, with timber-built porches, and three rectangular windows above.

Inside, there is a gallery on three sides supported on iron columns.

Former Maberly Chapel in 1990. It has since been renovated by a Sikh group

18 Former Bethany Hall

Nos 70–2 Barnsbury Road N1
(now Anna Scher Theatre)

Bethany Hall was built in 1934 as a Brethren meeting-house on the site of two terraced houses and an old corrugated-iron mission hall behind. The architect was A. W. Young. It has a red brick façade with a central round-arched window, recessed entrances and a cutaway parapet; there is a ground-floor hall. Bethany Hall closed in 1976 and is now a drama school.

19 Union Chapel

Compton Terrace N1   Grade II* listed

The rebuilding of the 'respectable and melancholy'[3] but inconveniently small Union Chapel of 1806 was mooted in 1871. From the start a prestige building seems to have been envisaged, for the deacons determined on a limited competition for designs, and to his

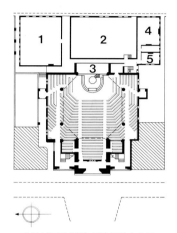

COMPTON AVENUE

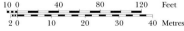

COMPTON TERRACE

1   Lecture hall (first floor)
2   Sunday school
3   Organ
4   Classroom
5   Vestry

Union Chapel. Based on a plan published in The Builder, *29 March 1878, and additional measurements taken 1991*

Union Chapel. Pulpit in 1991

chagrin their Surveyor of many years, Richard Lander (of Lander & Bedells), was not consulted.

Difficult negotiations with the freeholder, the Earl of Northampton, caused delay but in late 1874 the competition opened, Alfred Waterhouse acting as assessor.

The buildings, for a site enlarged by the annexation of the gardens of the next-door houses, were to be a chapel for at least 1,650, a lecture hall, Sunday school and other auxiliary rooms. All this, including fittings, was to cost no more than £15,000. Waterhouse said 'at the outset'[4] it could not be done. The final cost was £30,500.

The competitors included T. Roger Smith, T. Lewis Banks, Paull & Bickerdike, and a Coventry firm, T. & J. Steane. Lander & Bedells, and Finch Hill – a prominent member of the congregation – were also given a chance. John Sulman, who later designed Highbury Quadrant Congregational Church, was one of several architects who tried unsuccessfully to get on the list.

The winner was James Cubitt, author of *Church Design for Congregations: Its Development and Possibilities* (*see* Introduction). His success caused one of those rows which have soured so many architectural competitions. Banks complained that Cubitt's £18,750 estimate disqualified him. Others were angry too, though he was not alone in exceeding the estimate. Waterhouse calculated that, minus the tower, Cubitt's design could be built for within 10 per cent of £15,000, bringing it, just, into line with the competition rules. But as the notes for competitors had hinted at the desirability of a bell-tower, and it was such an integral feature of the design, criticism does seem justified.

The chapel was built in 1876–7 by L. H. & R. Roberts, of Rheidol Terrace, Islington, the tower being completed in 1889. A modified Greek cross, enclosing an octagon of alternate long and short sides formed by the gallery fronts, the plan was loosely based on that of Santa Fosca, Torcello. It was not the first Congregational church so planned and on such a scale. Paull & Bickerdike's Christ Church, Westminster Bridge Road (1873–5), seating 2,500, was in plan a Greek cross enclosing a similarly irregular octagon.

Instead of Romanesque, Cubitt looked principally to 13th-century French Gothic, using this style to particular effect in the tower. Faced in orange pressed brick (from Birmingham) and stone dressings, it is in three slightly diminishing stages with a cross-gabled top, surmounted by a shingled octagonal spirelet.

The chapel is faced internally in red Leicestershire pressed brick with Box stone dressings, panels of marble and onyx, and York stone piers at the angles of the octagon.

The gallery fronts are carried by pointed arcading with granite shafts, and segmental arches on the short sides. The tower, one of the arms of the Greek cross, provides seating on both levels. Despite the bulky masonry supports, virtually every seat has a good view of the pulpit. This, carved by Thomas Earp, is of Caen stone with alabaster, green marble and Mexican onyx. Screened off behind the pulpit is the organ, designed and built by Henry Willis.

Later additions include a piece of the Plymouth Rock, set over the Southeast doorway, and a memorial window by Lavers & Westlake to the Revd Thomas Allon (d. 1892), minister 1852–92.

(Opposite)
Union Chapel in 1991

Membership began to decline in the late 19th century, as the middle-class population of Highbury and Canonbury dwindled. By the 1970s, the chapel had become so dilapidated and underused that consideration was given to its demolition and replacement by a pastiche of the 1806 chapel. It remains in regular use for worship, and efforts are being made to promote viable alternative uses.

At the rear of the chapel, fronting Compton Avenue, a comparatively uninspired ancillary range contains the former Sunday school, a rectangular hall with narrow galleries on three sides, and lecture hall.

20 Blessed Sacrament Roman Catholic Church

Copenhagen Street N1

This church was opened in 1916 to serve Catholics living between the parishes of St John the Evangelist, Duncan Terrace, and St Aloysius, Somers Town. It was designed by R. L. Curtis and paid for by Mr (later Commendatore) James J. Hicks, KCSG.

A small building at first, occupying the site of two houses (a third was used for many years as the presbytery), it had a nearly square plan. It was greatly extended in 1957 by T. G. Birchall Scott. The original building is of purplish brick with some red brick and stone dressings and a tiled roof. Romanesque in style, standing flush to the pavement edge, it has a rather crowded symmetrical façade. The gabled central bay, flanked by doorways, has windows on four levels including the basement, and is crowned by what was originally a tall bell-gable.

(This page)
Blessed Sacrament Roman Catholic Church in 1990

(Opposite)
Union Chapel. West front in 1991

The entrances give on to small vestibules and staircases to an organ gallery. Disproportionately long, with an apsidal sanctuary, the church has a high collar-beam roof.

Movement in the upper walls led to most of the nave being closed off in 1989. It is proposed to build a new church and parish centre on the same site (Francis Wheal & Partners, architects).

The next-door presbytery, offices and sacristy were completed in 1967.

21 Cross Street Baptist Church

Cross Street N1

In 1851 a congregation of Baptists meeting at Islington Green Chapel in Providence Place, Upper Street (Gazetteer **32**), bought the present site for their new chapel. The Gothic-style building, opened on 29 June 1852, was designed by John Barnett, architect, a member of the congregation (*see* Notes on Demolished Buildings).

In 1856 a Sunday school hall, also by Barnett, was built at the rear, fronting Fowler Road. Early English in style, it is brick built with stone dressings and has an ornamental open truss roof. A second schoolroom was built in 1883 (Searle & Hayes, architects) at the rear of the caretaker's house adjoining the hall. The house is now a private residence and the school has been converted into a studio.

Bombed out in 1940, the congregation continued to meet in the hall until the completion of the new church in 1957. Plans to erect old folks' flats on the site of bombed houses adjoining the church fell through, giving the present building its wide frontage.

Designed by W. B. Attenbrow and built by W. J. Cearns Ltd of Stratford, E15, the new church is built on the foundations of the old. Of light brown brick with a pitched roof and side windows rising through low eaves, it is flanked by low wings comprising a youth hall and manse.

Cross Street Baptist Church. Former Sunday school hall in 1990

There is an open baptistery with a stepped parapet. On the wall behind, artificially lit, is a memorial window of *c*1882, salvaged from Highbury Hill Baptist Church.

22 Roman Catholic Church of Our Lady of Czestochowa and St Casimir

Devonia Road N1
(formerly New Church College)

New Church College was a school and national seminary for the New Jerusalem Church (Swedenborgians). The promoters of the scheme were Henry Bateman and Roger Crompton, who in 1845 formally instituted 'Emmanuel College'. It was intended that graduates of this college – the name was changed on the ground that use of the word Emmanuel was a breach of the Ten Commandments – would be eligible for matriculation to the University of London.

The originally intended site was near the New Church in Argyle Square. Building at Devonshire (now Devonia) Road, on

DEVONIA ROAD

1 Drawing-room
2 Priests' dining-room
3 Stairs to vestry and pulpit
4 Sanctuary
5 Chapel dedicated to Polish armed forces
6 Confessionals
7 Office

Roman Catholic Church of Our Lady of Czestochowa and St Casimir. From a survey made in 1991

Roman Catholic Church of Our Lady of Czestochowa and St Casimir in 1990

New Church College Chapel (now Roman Catholic Church of Our Lady of Czestochowa and St Casimir). Reredos in 1903. Photograph by Bedford Lemere

land leased from the developer Thomas Cubitt, began in 1852 with the northern wing. Designed by Edward Welch, this comprised a basement Sunday schoolroom, a mission hall of double-storey height, living accommodation on top and a staircase tower on the south side. In 1856 a gallery was added to the mission hall, designed eventually to be incorporated into a complete new floor.

By 1860 the project seemed ready to go ahead. Crompton had died, leaving £10,000 for 'maturing and extending'[5] the institution. Bateman announced the establishment of a school for day-pupils and boarders in the existing building. However, at its height there were only six scholars.

In 1865 new architects, Finch Hill & Paraire, drew up plans for the chapel and south wing, but there was still barely enough money and various economies had to be made. The main building work (by Dove Brothers) was done in the next two years, but it was not until 1879, when the reredos was installed, that the chapel was regarded as complete.

Since 1930, when the College moved to Woodford Green, the building has been the home of a Polish Roman Catholic mission, previously based at a former sailors' institute in Shadwell.

The building is of white brick with a stone façade, in convincingly collegiate Gothic. The gabled West front, faced in Kentish

(Opposite)
Roman Catholic Church of Our Lady of Czestochowa and St Casimir in 1990

Rag with ashlar dressings, has an arched recessed porch with a large Perpendicular window above and is flanked by staircase towers, buttressed and pinnacled. The wings are ashlar faced.

The church comprises a tall rectangular nave with an organ gallery at the West end. It is clad internally with limestone and has a dark-stained open timber roof. The South wall is pierced by arched openings giving on to a low-ceilinged side chapel (originally a schoolroom), dedicated to the Polish armed forces.

The church contains, somewhat altered, the Swedenborgians' Gothic-style reredos, designed by Alexander Payne and executed in Caen stone by Martyn & Emms of Cheltenham. Replete with New Church imagery and symbolism, the original centrepiece was a bas-relief of the objects of the Jewish tabernacle, set behind an ogee arch and framed by tapestry curtains ornamented with pomegranates. The whole was surmounted by a canopied niche, rising to a tall spire, containing a statue of Christ in the style of the Danish sculptor Bertel Thorwaldsen (1770–1844).

The most remarkable feature of the church is the series of stained glass windows made for it by the Polish artist Professor Adam Bunsch during the Second World War. Scenes of war illustrate the historic struggle for Polish sovereignty. One window (now reinstalled in an office in the south wing) depicts the Annunciation. Bunsch, a serving soldier, executed the glass at the

Roman Catholic Church of Our Lady of Czestochowa and St Casimir. Stained glass window in side chapel dedicated to Polish armed forces

works of Lowndes & Drury, the Glass House, Lettice Road, Fulham. Also by Bunsch is the painting of the Last Supper behind the altar. The stained glass in the clerestory and East window was supplied in 1952–3 by Stanley G. Higgins of Upper Berkeley Street.

The Stations of the Cross, by J. Z. Henelt, are bronze bas-reliefs made in 1945.

23 Roman Catholic Church of St John the Evangelist

Duncan Terrace N1   Grade II listed

Like Union Chapel, this church interrupts a terrace of houses to which it concedes nothing in style, scale or colour. Built of orange brick with stone dressings, it is Romanesque in style, with a gabled West front flanked by spired towers of unequal heights.

A Catholic school house was built nearby in Duncan Street in 1837, followed in 1839 by a small chapel. The present church, designed by J. J. Scoles, was built in 1842–3 to seat 2,000. Shortage of funds delayed its completion. The debt incurred was only paid off, and the building consecrated, in 1873; it was not until 1877 that the Southwest tower was given its additional stage and both spires were built. The side chapels were not fitted up for many years. The spires, originally leaded, were recovered in copper in the 1950s–60s.

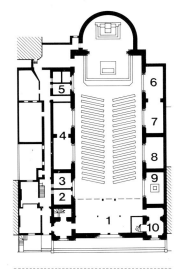

DUNCAN TERRACE

1 Narthex with organ gallery over
2 Waiting-room
3 Confessional
4 Chapel of Christ the King
5 Stores
6 Lady Chapel
7 Sacred Heart Chapel
8 Chapel of St Francis
9 Baptistery
10 Stairs to crypt

Roman Catholic Church of St John the Evangelist, and manse adjoining. Based on a survey drawing by Scott & Jaques, architects (1966, Diocese of Westminster Parish Buildings Section), Ordnance Survey (1894–6) and additional measurements taken 1991

Pugin castigated Scoles for his design, but not simply for not using Gothic. He saw St John's as the true successor to the medieval parish church of Islington (which had been rebuilt in 1751–4) and produced an alternative design showing 'St. Marie's, Islington, restored' – a sprawling country church which it would have been impossible to shoehorn into the terrace. Lamenting the absence of a 'good massive parochial tower,' he sneered that Scoles' church was 'built on the *all-front-principle* of Dissenters'.[6] But as *The Builder* pointed out, given the site, 'all front' was more or less the only option.

St John's was not completed as planned, with symmetrical towers, slender octagonal spires and corner spirelets. Nor was the intended rebuilding carried out of the priests' house adjoining, to have been in matching style with a central oriel.

The church comprises a broad nave with an apsidal sanctuary. Instead of aisles, Scoles placed a series of windowless rooms behind the nave arcades, for devotional chapels and confessionals, a scheme criticized by Pugin as 'extraordinary'.[7]

Inside, there have been several changes, including the blocking up of the apse windows. The hammerbeam roof, a remodelling of the original tie-beam trusses, was done *c*1901 during refurbishment by F. W. Tasker.

The decorations and furnishings include several interesting items, but the most important, frescoes in the apse by Edward Armitage depicting Jesus and the Apostles, the Holy Ghost, Moses

(This page)
Roman Catholic Church of St John the Evangelist. Sanctuary, c1895. From a photograph in the possession of the parish priest

(Opposite)
Roman Catholic Church of St John the Evangelist, c1895. From a photograph in the possession of the parish priest

Roman Catholic Church of St John the Evangelist in 1990

and Elias, have been obliterated. Also by Armitage are paintings in the chapel of St Francis, depicting SS Francis and Anthony and the institution of the Franciscan Order.

The statue of St Joseph in the Sacred Heart chapel, by Mayer & Co. of Munich, came from St Mary's, Horseferry Road, the parent church of Westminster Cathedral.

In 1977–8 the crypt was excavated and converted to make a youth centre (Joan Davis, architect).

Mrs Basil Holmes, in *The London Burial Grounds* (1896), records the existence of tombstones in the graveyard at the back. This has since been razed and incorporated into the playground of the school attached to the church.

24 Former Sandemanian meeting-house

No. 18A Furlong (formerly Albion) Road N1
(*now Leeson Hall*)

This small hall, an extension at the side of No. 18, was built *c*1886 by seceders from the Sandemanian meeting-house in Barnsbury Grove. It matches No. 18 with a rusticated stuccoed front, and has a central porch flanked by round-arched windows. Two small windows above were inserted when a first floor was added, some time after its closure in 1947.

It has been occupied by the local Conservative Association for many years.

25 Former Gifford Hall

Gifford Street N1
(now Keskidee Centre)

Gifford Hall was built in 1873. Originally a Congregational mission hall under the auspices of Offord Road Chapel (Gazetteer **28**), it also housed a Working Men's Institute and Club. It was later run by the Shaftesbury Society, becoming a West Indian youth club and cultural centre in the 1970s.

It is Gothic style, of stock brick with stone dressings and some polychrome brickwork. It has a tall, oddly proportioned gable front, the first floor, containing the main hall (now with additional floors put in), being narrower than the lower part of the building.

26 Christian meeting-room

No. 57 Islington Park Street N1

Hidden away down a roofed-in alley, and almost completely hemmed-in by buildings, No. 57 has no architectural pretensions. It has been in continual use for Christian meetings since it was opened by Brethren as Park Street Hall in 1874. Originally long and rather narrow, it was extended to its present nearly square plan in 1938, at which time the galleries on all sides and cinema-style seating for about 700 worshippers were installed.

No. 57 Islington Park Street (Park Street Hall) in 1990

The plainness of the hall and absence of any architectural focal point, other than an open central area, reflect the simple nature of services held, which are non-sacramental gospel meetings with unaccompanied hymn-singing.

27 Trinity Presbyterian Church

No. 60 Northchurch Road N1
(former manse)

Trinity Presbyterian Church next door, now demolished, was in the Borough of Hackney. It was built in 1856–7 on a lease from the De Beauvoir Town Estate to replace the Scots Church in London Wall, whose congregation was the oldest Presbyterian church in London. The minister already lived nearby, in Englefield Road.

Trinity Church was designed by T. E. Knightley in limited competition, and built by E. Clarke of Tottenham. In Decorated Gothic style, it comprised an oblong nave with very narrow aisles and a tower with a brick and stone broach spire (dismantled 1936). It had a hammerbeam roof. Closed in 1934/5, it was sold to the Brotherhood Church.[8]

The manse, also by Knightley, was built in 1859. It is distinguished by eaves brackets, Gothic tracery in the sash-windows, and steep hipped roofs to the front bay windows and side wing. A lecture hall, now demolished, was built at the rear in the 1880s.

28 Former Congregational chapel

Offord Road N1

Offord Road Chapel was built in 1856–7 for breakaway members of Caledonian Road Congregational Chapel, who had been worshipping for the previous two years at Twyford Hall nearby in Twyford Street.

Like many Victorian churches, it was built on borrowed money. When completed little over a third of the cost had been raised by subscription, although a further tenth had been given by the London Congregational Chapel Building Society. It could seat 800 adults and 200 children. So big a building was not needed. The *Daily News* religious census of 1902–3 found morning services attended by only 130 and the afternoon congregation little larger. It closed in 1916, the congregation merging with Union Chapel, and has since been in commercial use, latterly as a decorators' materials warehouse.

It was designed by Lander & Bedells and built by Dove Brothers. Early English in style, of white brick with orange brick and Bath stone dressings and a leaded pyramidal roof, it has a projecting gabled front with a triple-lancet window, flanked by turrets and gabled porches – one porch now removed. The spires and other decorative features have been taken down.

Like the slightly earlier Harecourt Chapel, it has a basically octagonal plan and was originally galleried. In the basement were vestries and a schoolroom for about 500 children.

(Opposite)
Former Congregational chapel, Offord Road, in 1990

29 King's Cross Welsh Tabernacle

Pentonville Road N1   Grade II listed
(former Congregational church)

This has been a Welsh Congregational church since 1889. It was built in 1853–4, with some financial aid from the London Congregational Chapel Building Society, to the design of Henry Hodge of Kentish Town.

In Early Decorated style with tall two-light windows, it comprises a broad oblong nave and basement schoolrooms. It is brick built, faced in Kentish Rag rubble with dressings of Caen stone and, for windows and doorways, Ransome's patent siliceous stone.

Extensive alterations were carried out in 1904 by Alfred Conder. As built, the Pentonville Road entrance was through a short Northwest tower which had a pyramidal roof and lucarnes on each face. The remodelling involved the building of a double-gabled porch, faced in faience. The tower was lowered and given a gable front. Other changes included the insertion of large dormers, replacing spherical triangular windows in gables over the middle bays.

Inside, Conder's work involved the creation of an entrance lobby with a glazed screen to the church, new staircases, and minister's and deacons' vestries behind the pulpit. The interior, an impressive space with a high open timber roof, is galleried all round with seating on three sides and an organ at the East end beneath a large wheel window. The gallery, fitted in 1857 and extended in 1904, when the organ was installed, has a pitch-pine balcony front ornamented with blind Gothic arcading and is supported on cast-iron columns. The pulpit and 'Big Seat' for the deaconry are in similar style.

The roof has hammerbeams set well above the feet of the rafters to provide clearance for the gallery. The spandrels to the arched braces are pierced by trefoils and the ends of the hammerbeams are capped with shields pierced by quatrefoils. Angel heads, of artificial stone, decorate the corbels.

The entrance lobby contains several memorials, including one to John Brees, wholesale ironmonger (d. 1851), removed from Fetter Lane Chapel, the former home of the present congregation.

Howell Elvert Lewis, the hymnist and poet, was minister of the church from 1904 to 1940.

King's Cross Welsh Tabernacle, Pentonville Road front in 1990

King's Cross Welsh Tabernacle in 1990

The basement is now occupied by Service Away From Home, a youth opportunities organization.

30 Grimaldi Park House

Pentonville Road N1
(site of St James's Pentonville, formerly Pentonville Chapel)

Grimaldi Park House stands on the site of St James's Church, demolished in 1983–4, the façade of which it replicates.

St James's Church was built in 1787–8 as a proprietary chapel serving the new residential district of Pentonville. It was built on a perpetually renewable twenty-one-year lease granted by Henry Penton. There were fifty-five proprietors, one of whom, the architect Aaron Hurst, designed the building, originally called Pentonville Chapel. Hurst also designed houses to adjoin the chapel, but these were not built.

Penton had intended a chapel of ease to Clerkenwell parish church to be built at Pentonville in 1777, getting a clause inserted in the local Paving Act empowering the Commissioners of Paving to build such a chapel with the vicar's approval. But the plan fell through because of a disagreement with the vicar over the payment of the minister's stipend.

Pentonville Chapel opened in 1788 as a Dissenting chapel, but services were as close to the Anglican form as possible. A couple of years later, the residents of Pentonville opposed a Bill to enable the Commissioners for rebuilding the parish church to raise additional money, until a clause was inserted obliging them to buy Pentonville Chapel. The proprietors were duly bought out, and in June 1791 the chapel and grounds were consecrated by the Bishop of London. The chapel was given its own parish in 1854.

Pentonville Chapel was oblong in plan, galleried on three sides, with an apsidal sanctuary between lobbies leading off the rear entrances. The Pentonville Road front was in three bays, the outer bays with round-headed doorways and windows over. The centrepiece, with sparing Adam-style decoration in Coade stone, comprised a doorway with a large elliptical-headed window above, flanked by paired Ionic pilasters carrying a low pediment with an oval clock. There was an open-sided cupola with an ogee dome.

In 1933 the church was made smaller by taking down the outer bays to ground-floor level, thus getting rid of the side galleries. The architect was T. Murray Ashford.

St James's was long considered one of the prettiest London churches. Ian Nairn described its yellow bricks as 'among the mellowest and duskiest in London'.[9] Services ceased in 1972. In 1978 the church was declared redundant. It was gutted by fire in 1983.

The idea of building offices with a facsimile façade was first suggested in 1981. Grimaldi Park House, by Allies and Morrison, architects, was completed in 1990. It is occupied by Courtaulds Textiles.

The churchyard, closed in 1853 and laid out as a public garden in 1897, contains the grave of Joseph Grimaldi (1779–1837), the famous clown. Aaron Hurst and Henry Penton (d. 1812) are also buried there.

31 Former Claremont Chapel

No. 44A Pentonville Road   Grade II listed

Claremont Chapel was built in 1818–19 with the support of Thomas Wilson, who financed a number of Independent chapels, including Paddington Chapel, Hoxton Chapel and Craven Chapel in Marylebone. It closed in 1899, after some years of decline and poverty. It was altered and reopened as the Central London Mission by the London Congregational Union in 1902. Claremont Hall, as it became, was greatly added to during the next few years. In the 1960s the whole of the mission activities were concentrated in the newer buildings and the chapel was let commercially. Occupied until recently by a firm of dental equipment suppliers, it was reopened in September 1991 as the new national centre of the Crafts Council.

The architect of the chapel was probably William Wallen, who charged for surveying in connection with the new building. But it is interesting to note that Andrew Blyth, surveyor, of Goswell Road, was one of the small band of original members. He was probably the father of John Blyth, architect of Northampton Tabernacle (now the Roman Catholic Church of SS Peter and Paul, Gazetteer 1), who later practised at the same address.

Claremont Chapel, Pentonville Road, c1860. Lithograph by H. Greenwood. Finsbury Library

The building was at first rather plain. It was said of Thomas Wilson that 'the chapels he built in London, though well adapted to hold large audiences, have bare and unsightly exteriors…and even Craven Chapel, the largest and most costly of the whole, has only a very meagre approach to an architectural character'. [10] Although the shell of the building remains largely intact, it has been gutted and the front has undergone successive changes.

The façade is Classical in style, stuccoed, with large round-headed windows and a portico with paired Ionic columns. It is in three bays, the middle bay, with the main entrance, brought forward and pedimented. This basic layout is original, the main change being the enlargement (1902) of the side doorways.

The front was not at first stuccoed; this was done in about 1860, and such ornamentation as the cornices over the upper windows also dates from that time. Various improvements made in 1854–5 included, at the suggestion of the architect, Henry Owen of Great Marlborough Street, the building of a balustraded terrace on either side of the entrance steps. Owen's arrangement was subsequently altered, but something resembling it has been built as part of the recent refurbishment of the building for the Crafts Council. The Neoclassical railings and gatepiers are original.

Inside, an oval gallery ran round the chapel, so that a number of seats faced the minister's back. This end of the gallery was removed in 1860 and the pulpit relocated. As altered, the chapel could seat 1,500.

The alterations made in 1902 (by the architects Barnes-Williams, Ford & Griffin, and the builder John Greenwood) included the installation of fireproof staircases, replacing the original narrow timber stairs from the side doors to the gallery. Vestries and a Sunday school at the rear of the chapel were rebuilt to provide a lecture hall, classrooms and kitchen. Property to the north, fronting White Lion Street, was acquired and in 1906–10 a new building, the Claremont Institute, was erected on the site (Gazetteer **37**).

In 1847 a small school was built in connection with Claremont Chapel in King's Cross Road (Gazetteer **15**).

32 Former Providence Chapel

Providence Place N1

Islington Green Chapel, as it was called until the 1860s, was built *c*1832 as a chapel or school by the Revd Robert Stodhard, a Countess of Huntingdon's Connexion minister. He let the chapel but ran a school in a detached vestry room at the rear, which in 1838 he opened as a place of worship called Islington Tabernacle. The Tabernacle was taken over in 1853 by Strict Baptists who later moved to the main building – which had been used successively by Calvinistic Methodists, Baptists and Wesleyans – and in 1888 took the name Providence with them to a new chapel in Highbury Place (Gazetteer **51**). The Tabernacle was demolished and the old chapel, called Providence Hall, remained in use by Baptists until *c*1931 when it was acquired by the British Legion. After many years in commercial or industrial use, latterly as a dress factory, it was partly rebuilt and converted into offices in 1990–1.

Former chapel, Providence Place, in 1990

It is a plain brick building down an alley off Upper Street. Classical style, with a slightly battered doorway, it had, before the recent alterations, two squat round-arched windows on the upper level and ornamentation in relief brickwork.

33 Paget Memorial Mission Hall

Randell's Road N1

In 1911 two houses in an unremarkable 1880s terrace in Randell's Road, in the hinterland of King's Cross goods yard, were converted into a mission hall. The hall was built in memory of Violet Mary Paget (1856–1908), one of the many children of Lord Alfred Paget and granddaughter of the 1st Marquess of Anglesey, Wellington's second-in-command at Waterloo.

From 1887 to 1889 Violet worked as a deaconess with the Mildmay Mission. As part of her work, based at St Michael's, Bingfield Street, nearby, she ran Bible classes for men. There are conflicting traditions about where the classes were held, but the evidence suggests the front room of 26 Randell's Road. The house, in common with others in the terrace, was a lodging house by 1890 and remained so until the creation of the mission hall.

In 1889 Violet Paget married the Revd Douglas Sholto Campbell Douglas, later Lord Blythswood, vicar of St Silas's, Glasgow. Living at Douglas Support, Coatbridge, she continued to be involved in mission work.

Reading of her death, in June 1908, one of her former pupils got in touch with Lord Blythswood and subsequently traced many fellow scholars for a reunion in the old Bible-class room. The meeting gave rise to a memorial mission to revive Violet's work, funded by an endowment from Blythswood and overseen by the Evangelization Society.

The freehold of Nos 18–26 (even) Randell's Road was acquired and plans to convert Nos 22–4 into a mission hall were drawn up by Arthur Beresford Pite. No more suitable architect could have been found: Pite himself was a lay preacher and exegetist, whose activities included missionary work at Wormwood Scrubs prison.

The hall was opened on 20 May 1911. Rising through two floors and extending over the back yards of the houses, it is oblong with canted corners at the East end. There are large half-round windows at back and front. Externally it could hardly be plainer or less calculated to hint at the style of the interior – a complete contrast to another terrace conversion by Pite, Pagani's Restaurant in Great Portland Street, exotically ornamented with female figures and flowing patterns in glazed tilework (1904–5; destroyed in the Second World War). Pite's original drawings, dated September 1910, show an even plainer treatment, with the upper windows of the houses unaltered. As it is, the front window is largely obscured by the organ, standing on a bow-fronted gallery.

Entered unobtrusively from a small lobby at the side, the hall is startingly furnished with dark carved wood and brightly coloured pots and vases. Most of this extraordinary collection, which includes some decidedly pagan imagery, is reputed to have come from Blythswood's home at Douglas Support. The house was extensively damaged by fire only a few days after Violet's death.

Paget Memorial Mission Hall in 1990

70

The walls have dark wooden panelling to half-height, in the form of blind Gothic arcading, ornamented with decorative plasterwork. Drops of fruit, flowers, seed cones and pods hang from cartouches with the monogram VP. Stencilled gold violets form a frieze along the top. Behind the minister's platform, the panelling rises to a pediment with coats of arms. The prayer over the East window is the same as that which decorated the Mildmay Mission Conference Hall.

The strongest architectural element is the mock-Tudor roof of black trusses and black-and-white battened ceiling. The timbers are matt in finish and the ornamental touches in the form of curly brackets and pendants are of simple fretwork.

Nos 26 and 28 were fitted up with a reading-room and other ancillary rooms, including accommodation for the missioner and his family. The lower floors of Nos 18 and 20 were later made into a drill hall. The front room of No. 26, called the Leader's Room after 'Our Leader' Violet Paget, contains mementoes of her and Lord Blythswood, including prayer books, Bibles and a Minton breakfast set, a wedding gift from Queen Victoria.

Since 1927 the hall has been run by the London City Mission.

(Opposite)
Paget Memorial Mission Hall in 1990

(This page)
Paget Memorial Mission Hall. Detail of sanctuary

34 Harecourt United Reformed Church

St Paul's Road N1

Harecourt Congregational Chapel, as it was originally called, was burned out in 1982 and stood in ruins for several years. A new church, designed by Hodson Rivers, architects, was still under construction in December 1991. A plain yellow-brick building, this will comprise a rectangular nave seating 150, with a church hall above. The design of the old chapel (*see* Notes on Demolished Buildings) will be recalled by an octagonal reception and ancillary wing.

35 Former Islington Chapel

Upper Street N1   Grade II listed

Former Islington Chapel, Upper Street, in 1990

In 1788 John Ives, a local blacksmith inspired by the preaching of Jeremiah Garrett at Islington, set up a congregation in association with Garrett which, begun in a burst of fervour, had a fraught history.

A chapel was built in Church (now Gaskin) Street (*see* Notes on Demolished Buildings), but was not finished until 1793, when it was leased to George Welch of Colebrooke Row and let by him to Thomas Wills, a former minister of the Countess of Huntingdon's Connexion and a relation by marriage of the Countess. It was taken over in 1800 by the Revd Evan Jones. In 1814–15, during Jones' ministry, a new chapel was built nearby in Upper Street (*see* Notes on Demolished Buildings). Under Jones the congregation grew, but there was controversy. Jones was making money from the boom and had also set up a commercial graveyard called New Bunhill Fields Cemetery in a garden adjoining the old chapel.

Bickering and secession plagued the congregation for decades and numbers fell. During a period of revival in the 1880s the Metropolitan Board of Works compulsorily purchased the site for road-widening and the chapel was demolished.

The present building, occupying part of the old site, was built in 1887–8. It is in Queen Anne style, built of red brick with gauged brick and Portland stone dressings and a red tiled roof. The architects were Bonella & Paull, the builders Patman & Fotheringham. Most of the ironwork, including the area railings, entrance gates and balustrades over the entrances, was made by the St Pancras Iron Company.

The Upper Street front, flanked by porches and a staircase wing on the left, rises to a lofty gable with a large oriel window. The roof is crowned by a hexagonal cupola.

As completed, the building comprised a large galleried chapel with a wagon roof of elliptical arch section, basement school, and ancillary rooms. The chapel, divided into nave and aisles by the columns supporting the gallery, could hold a thousand people. The original colour scheme was predominantly dark olive green, relieved by the gallery front in white.

The main schoolroom could be divided into a number of compartments by means of low folding screens which, when closed, formed a dado round the walls. Thus nearly thirty classes could be held under scrutiny by a single superintendent.

Closed in 1979, the congregation merging with that of Claremont U.R.C. (Gazetteer **37**), the chapel is now converted to recording studios and offices.

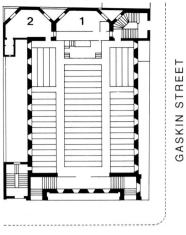

UPPER STREET

1 Vestry
2 Deacons' vestry

Islington Chapel, Upper Street. Based on a plan published in Building News, 20 December 1889

36 Unity Church

Upper Street N1

The history of Unity Church goes back to 1732 when a Unitarian chapel was built in Carter Lane, City. The present building replaces a church of 1860–2, built when the congregation moved to Islington, which was destroyed in 1941 (*see* Notes on Demolished Buildings). It was built in 1958 to the rear of the old site, which is occupied by the London Fire Brigade.

A simple brick building with square picture windows, pitched copper-covered roof and small saddleback-roofed tower, it was designed, by Kenneth Tayler, as a 'dual-purpose' church. The nave or hall is a plain room with a concrete portal frame roof. A folding screen conceals the chancel when not in use.

Communicating with the church is a hall (part of the original building) and the Preston Memorial Rooms, built in 1906–7 in memory of Joseph Thomas Preston (1819–1904), a prominent Unitarian and Past Master of the Carpenters' Company. The building, fronting Florence Street, comprises kitchen, schoolroom and caretaker's apartment. It is tall and narrow with a mansard roof, built of stock brick with red brick dressings in a basically neo-Georgian style; the doorway has a segmental stone arch, heavily moulded. It was designed by Howard Chatfeild-Clarke and built by C. P. Roberts.

37   Islington Claremont United Reformed Church

White Lion Street N1
(formerly Claremont Institute)

Rooms, replacing old schoolrooms, were built on to the rear of Claremont Chapel (Gazetteer **31**) in 1902 and in 1906 these were

Islington Claremont United Reformed Church in 1990

extended as part of a new building fronting White Lion Street, the Claremont Institute. Two additional bays (on the right) were added in 1910. The completed building, designed by Alfred Conder, has a balanced rather than symmetrical façade in Queen Anne style, faced in red brick with a glazed brick plinth and stone dressings. The entrance is through a recessed porch with wrought-iron gates beneath a large segmental pediment. The front, three floors high, is crowned by a prominent concrete parapet enclosing a roof garden.

The Claremont Institute comprised various club rooms including rooms for billiards and music, refreshment bars, crèche, dispensary, kitchens and living accommodation.

It is still used as a social centre and part has been converted to use for worship. In addition to those of the United Reformed Church, services are also held by the All Souls Pentecostal Church. The worship room contains furnishings, including a marble font, from Islington Chapel (Gazetteer **35**). Several items were acquired by Claremont when King's Weigh House Chapel in Duke Street, Mayfair, was sold in the 1960s, including a jewelled brass eagle lectern of 1899, later stolen.

38 First Born Church of the Living God

White Lion Street N1
(former Mount Zion Chapel Sunday School)

Run in connection with Mount Zion Baptist Chapel (now Angel Baptist Church, Gazetteer **3**), the Sunday school was built at a cost of just over £2,000 and opened in February 1897. The site, although likened to a 'waste howling wilderness',[11] contained two old houses, and the building probably incorporates much of their structure. Set behind tall area railings, it has a somewhat forbidding air. Brick built, it has a sheer front dominated by rectangular windows with stone mullions and transoms and heavy stone surrounds. The main entrance doors have rectangular fanlights with cusped heads.

The building comprises a main hall, rising through basement, ground- and first-floor levels, two floors of ancillary and living rooms above, and a lantern-roofed ground-floor hall forming a rear extension (now thrown open to the main hall and fitted with a false ceiling). The main hall has a gallery at the end away from the street (formerly the East end – the orientation has now been reversed) and a narrow side gallery. The galleries have conventional decorative balustrading of cast iron; a pull-down shutter enables the large gallery, intended for separate use as an infant's classroom, to be closed off.

Since 1967 the building has been occupied by a Pentecostal church, now called the First Born Church of the Living God.

N4

39 Christadelphian hall

No. 48A Blackstock Road N4
(former Finsbury Park Room)

A proposal to erect a meeting-house here was rejected by the
Metropolitan Board of Works in 1879, but a revised plan for a
warehouse by the same applicant, H. Parsons (probably Henry
Parsons, architect of Brixton Public Market, 1876), was approved
a few months later. This 'warehouse' was registered as a Brethren
hall in 1885 and appears to be the building used since 1932 by
Christadelphians. From *c*1915 to 1932 it was a clothing factory.

Altered at one or other times, is a plain brick-built hall down an
alley off Blackstock Road.

40 Former Fifth Church of Christ Scientist

Blythwood Road N4

This former church, now a community centre, was built in 1962
for a long-established local congregation. The architect was G. H.
Gatley, a church member. Brick built, it comprises a hall with a
concrete shell roof of shallow barrel-vaulted section, entered from
a large flat-roofed foyer at the side.

*Former Fifth Church of Christ Scientist in
1990*

41 Holly Park Methodist Church

Crouch Hill N4

Holly Park Methodist Church was built in 1881–2, replacing an iron church opened in 1875 by Sir Francis Lycett. The architect was Elijah Hoole, who lived locally and was a member of the congregation. Hoole also designed a Sunday school and lecture hall, built at the back of the church in 1886. A Gothic-style building of red brick with stone dressings, the church had a centralized plan based on a Greek cross. There were galleries on three sides, supported on stone columns, with stone balcony fronts. A clock tower and spire were added in 1910. It must always have been too large: able to seat 1,000, it was only quarter full at the time of the *Daily News* religious census in 1902–3.

Only the rather dismal-looking ancillary building survives. The church was pulled down *c*1961 and a 192-seater replacement put up, together with a block of flats, opened in May 1962. Built of buff-coloured brick with a reinforced-concrete frame, the new church has a raised ground floor, the front portion projecting and carried on piers. The roof is flat with sloping sides, giving a truncated gable front which is ornamented with a dark brick cross in relief. The architect was Michael Pipe.

42 Former Congregational mission hall

Nos 27–9 Lennox Road N4

The pair of houses and hall at rear on the corner of Lennox Road and Fonthill Mews were built in 1884 as a mission of New Court Congregational Church. The architects were Searle & Hayes, the builders Wilson & Exton of Aldersgate Street.

The premises, now converted to secular use, were occupied by Elim Pentecostalists from 1951 to 1977.

43 Former Sunday school, Finsbury Park Congregational Church

Playford (formerly Palmerston) Road N4

Finsbury Park Congregational Church and School were built in 1882–3 by John Woodward of Finsbury to the designs of Charles Henry Searle. The Romanesque-style church, built of red brick with blue brick plinths and Bath stone dressings, had a prominent clock tower, domed and turreted. An unusual feature was the placing of a hall (seating 900) over the church, rather than in the basement. The church itself, galleried on all sides, could seat 1,300. It closed in 1939; the site is now occupied by a service station.

The comparatively perfunctory ancillary wing, now a dress factory, has a gabled front with a large wheel window over the entrance. The first floor comprised a lecture hall.

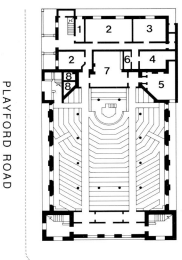

PLAYFORD ROAD

SEVEN SISTERS ROAD

1 Cloakroom
2 Classroom
3 Infants' room
4 Tea-making room
5 Minister's vestry
6 Store
7 Deacons' vestry
8 Ventilation shaft

Finsbury Park Congregational Church (largely demolished). From a plan published in Congregational Year Book *(1882)*

44   Elim Pentecostal Church and Newcourt Centre

Regina Road N4
(former New Court Congregational Church)

This building, with a spiky multi-faceted roof of copper and glass on timber framing, was designed by John Diamond as a smaller replacement for New Court Congregational Church in Tollington Park nearby (Gazetteer **47**). Built at a cost of £38,000, it was opened in October 1961.

It is a low brick-built ground-floor range comprising a church, a large hall behind with a low-pitched portal roof, and ancillary rooms. The church roof is a tall pentagonal pyramid with raised flat-topped triangular wings making a star-shaped plan. Between the points of the star the roof is flat, partly carried on pillars, the room itself being broadly rectangular with a triangular sanctuary.

The congregation having continued to decline, the church was closed in 1976. Since 1977 it has been occupied by Elim Pentecostalists who had previously met at the former New Court mission in Lennox Road (Gazetteer **42**).

Elim Pentecostal Church, Regina Road, in 1990

45 Zoar Hall

Tollington Park N4

Zoar Hall was built in 1887 as a Sunday school for a Strict Baptist congregation formed in 1851 which had been worshipping in John Street (now Wedmore Street), Upper Holloway. An intended chapel was never built and services continued in the schoolroom.

It is a small building of stock brick with orange brick dressings, gable fronted with a small lean-to porch. Since 1959 it has belonged to Tollington Park Baptist Church.

46 Tollington Park Baptist Church

Tollington Park N4

This chapel was built in 1908 as the Spurgeon Memorial Baptist Chapel for a congregation formed in Hornsey Road in 1893. It was designed by E. Douglas Hoyland, architect and surveyor.

Constructed of hollow terracotta blocks, it comprises an oblong aisled nave with a pitched roof and lean-to aisle roofs of slightly shallower pitch. Above the entrance is a large segmental-arched window of five lights with cusped heads. Two sentry-box-like porches were demolished in 1972 when the church hall, by K. C. White & Partners, architects, was added.

The chapel is in six bays, the first two of which were cut off by a glazed partition when the hall was built, to provide a foyer. It has three-light side windows and large dormers. Unplastered, white painted, it is a simple interior given interest by the roof structure. The hammerbeam nave roof, carried on iron columns acting as arcade posts, has shaped hammer-braces, arched braces with ornamental bosses and vertical struts in the spandrels. It is reinforced with iron ties.

A baptistery is concealed beneath the communion platform.

Tollington Park Baptist Church in 1990

47 St Mellitus's Roman Catholic Church

Tollington Park N4
(formerly New Court Congregational Church)

Grade II listed

New Court Congregational Church was built in 1870–1. The congregation had been founded in 1662 in Bridges Street, Covent Garden, moving from there in 1696 to premises in Russell Court off Drury Lane. The first New Court Chapel was built in 1705 in Carey Street. Like many early Nonconformist chapels, it tried to be inconspicuous, but despite its obscurely placed site it was twice attacked by mobs and its contents burnt in Lincoln's Inn Fields.

The move to Tollington Park was occasioned by the compulsory purchase of the Carey Street site in 1865 for the building of the Law Courts. C. G. Searle, the architect of the new building and a deacon of the church, was no doubt one of the advocates of the new location. He lived nearby in Tollington Villas. The new church, and basement schoolroom, built at a cost of £10,500 (including £1,500 for the site), opened in September 1871.

In 1959 the building was sold to Roman Catholics who had been worshipping in a hall in Eversleigh Street and new premises were built in Regina Road (Gazetteer **44**).

St Mellitus's Roman Catholic Church in 1990

A grandiose Classical building, seating more than 1,000, it is built of white brick with stone dressings. The front has a tetrastyle portico of giant Corinthian columns with a pedimented roof, the order being continued in pilasters along the sides.

The interior – a rectangular nave with a gallery on three sides and a high coved and coffered ceiling – remains essentially intact. Internal changes include the removal of the original ornate bow-fronted pulpit, and the partitioning of part of the ground floor to make counselling-rooms and a 'cry-room' for worshippers with babies. Two memorial windows remain at gallery level; others were re-installed in the successor building in Regina Road.

Partial reconstruction of the upstairs and downstairs lobbies in 1884 enabled ninety additional seats to be fitted, bringing the total seating capacity to 1,340. But the early success of the church, stimulated by two exceptionally gifted ministers and the rising prosperity of the district, did not last. By the early 20th century capacity congregations were a thing of the past and the church went into a steady decline, culminating in dissolution. The building is now too large for the present Roman Catholic congregation.

At the rear of the church, contemporary with it, is a substantial ancillary wing containing rooms designed as vestries, classrooms and a hall for weekday services.

St Mellitus's Roman Catholic Church in 1990

N5

48 Former Wesleyan Methodist chapel

Gillespie Road N5

Built in 1878 as a mission chapel of Finsbury Park Methodist Church,[1] this is a plain Gothic-style chapel of stock brick with stone dressings, raised on a deep semi-basement (originally schoolrooms). The gabled front has a triple-lancet window, flanked by entrances up flights of steps. The architect was probably F. W. Boreham, who designed the parent church and was responsible for the enlargement of the chapel in 1884.

In commercial use since its closure c1933, it is now a warehouse. A complete first floor, replacing a timber gallery on iron columns, has been inserted.

Former Wesleyan Methodist chapel, Gillespie Road, in 1990

49 Former Highbury Grove Chapel

No. 18 Highbury Grove N5

Highbury Grove Chapel, or Highbury Chapel, was built c1793. The prime mover in its construction seems to have been the Revd Hugh Worthington (1752–1813). Worthington, minister of Salters' Hall in the City, lived nearby in Highbury Place. One of the great preachers of his day, he was remembered for 'his upright posture, his piercing eye, his bold and decisive tone, his pointed finger, the interest he gave to what he delivered, and the entire nothingness of what he often said'.[2]

In 1796 the chapel closed and was not used again until 1799, when a group of local residents founded the Evangelical Union Church there. After a few years, the congregation outgrew the inconvenient and 'ill-built'[3] chapel and in 1806 a replacement was built in Compton Terrace, the predecessor of the present Union Chapel.

The old chapel was converted to a dwelling house shortly afterwards. A resident for many years was Sir Francis Lycett, a leading lay Methodist, closely involved in the building of many chapels, who died there in 1880. Lycett is commemorated by a bust in Wesley's Chapel, City Road.

It is a stucco-fronted, Classical-style building. Cromwell mentions 'a domed skylight in the centre of the roof'[4] as being one of the original features; there is a circular skylight over the staircase today. The house has been altered in the present century. A carriageway has been carved through one side, and most of the stucco ornamentation, including brackets and cornices over the windows, has gone. Nos 16, 18 and 20 were built as a terrace, but the original effect is now lost, for No. 16 has been demolished (the party wall is now covered by a mural painted in 1986–7 by Dave Bangs, depicting *Wild Islington*) and No. 20 has been largely rebuilt.

No. 18 is now a local authority residential establishment for young persons.

50 Roman Catholic Church of St Joan of Arc

Highbury Park N5

St Joan of Arc Church occupies the site of a Carmelite convent founded in 1918, and replaces a hut (now the church hall) in Kelross Road which had served as a church since 1920. It was built in 1960–2 by Whyatt Builders Ltd of Streatham, who also built the school adjoining in 1963. The presbytery and offices, built by Dove Brothers, were completed in 1964. The architect of the whole complex was Stanley C. Kerr Bate of Walters & Kerr Bate.

The church, seating 760, is spaciously planned in a style described by the architect as 'modernised Gothic'.[5] A low-eaved pitched roof and deep buttresses give it an almost triangular section. There is a large triangular-headed window in the gabled West front, closely mullioned in the manner of the Perpendicular style but with no attempt at tracery. A tall North tower, slender but with deep oblique buttresses, and a pyramidal spire, make a notable local landmark. The spire is fitted with a radioactive lightning conductor, reportedly the first of its kind in this country.

The church is built of brick, faced externally in Dutch two-inch bricks of soft orange-yellow hues with dressings of Bath and Clipsham stone. The roof is tiled and the spire copper covered.

The entrance is through a narthex – with an organ loft above – screened from the body of the church by a glazed partition. Steps lead down into the nave. Dominating the interior is a series of rendered eighteen-inch brick-built ribs supporting the nave roof. They take the form of parabolic arches springing from ground level and rising high into the open roof space. The flat tops of the ribs carry queen-trussed collar beams. Broad arched openings to

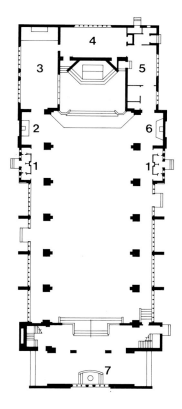

1 Confessionals
2 Sacred Heart Chapel
3 Lady Chapel
4 Priests' Sacristy
5 Boys' Sacristy
6 St Joan of Arc Chapel
7 Font

Roman Catholic Church of St Joan of Arc, showing intended internal arrangement. From a plan by Stanley C. Kerr Bate (1960, Diocese of Westminster Parish Buildings Section)

the aisles and generous windows at ground and clerestory levels offset the massive presence of the roof structure. Taken as a whole, the church (which seats 760) represents a thoroughly successful solution to the problem of filling a long and narrow site, the shape of which was dictated by the site requirements of the school.

The sanctuary, flanked at the front by ambos and small transeptal chapels, is defined at the rear by oblique wing-walls on either side of the altar. Behind the chapels are sacristies and a Lady Chapel respectively: the Lady Chapel, looking onto the sanctuary through plate glass, was designed to accommodate mothers with babies.

Furnishings include an electrically lit perspex statue of St Joan, made in 1962 by an Hungarian sculptor, Arthur Fleischmann. A wooden statue of Our Lady and Child was carved for the church by Ferdinand Stuflesser in 1962. Two further statues by Stuflesser, of St Thérèse of Lisieux and St Joseph the Worker, and Child, were obtained through Green Shield stamps.

To the right of the steps leading into the nave is a baptistery, decorated with fibreglass mock-marble bas-reliefs, fitted up in memory of Lodovico Parisi (d. 1966).

(This page and opposite)
Roman Catholic Church of St Joan of Arc in 1990

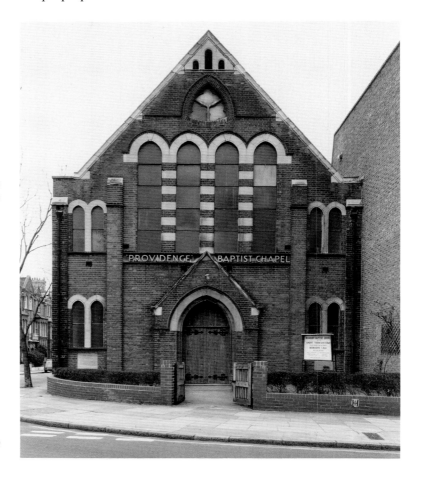

BAALBEC ROAD

HIGHBURY PLACE

1 Pulpit
2 Baptistery

10   0   10   20   30 Feet
2   0   10 Metres

Providence Baptist Chapel (Highbury Baptist Church). From a survey made in 1991

51 Providence Baptist Chapel

Highbury Place N5
(Highbury Baptist Church)

This Strict Baptist chapel was built in 1887 to replace a small chapel in Providence Place (Gazetteer **32**). Early English in style, of red brick with stone dressings, it was designed by C. J. Bentley. It was built, for £2,245, by a Grantham builder named Hockley.

Excepting the windows, blasted by bombing in the Second World War, and the creation of a new vestibule at the West end, it is little altered since late Victorian times. With its high hammer-beam roof, it must have been bleak and barn-like at first, but after a few years the gallery was installed. This runs along the sides and back and is entered via the entrance lobby or the first-floor vestry room at the other end. It is supported by iron columns and has a decorative iron-railed balustrade. The high-level pulpit (disused, as is the gallery) has similar ironwork. On the wall behind, a *trompe l'oeil* banner in blue and gold proclaims THE LORD OF HOSTS IS WITH US/THE GOD OF JACOB IS OUR REFUGE.

The ground floor is raked; a baptistery is concealed beneath the pulpit platform.

(This page and top opposite) Providence Baptist Chapel (Highbury Baptist Church) in 1990

52 Highbury Quadrant Congregational Church

Highbury Quadrant N5

Highbury Quadrant Congregational Church, built in 1880–2, was a Leviathan among local churches. It replaced a temporary building put up in 1878 for a new congregation formed as an off-shoot of Harecourt Congregational Chapel, St Paul's Road (Gazetteer **34**). Designed in competition by John Sulman and built by Jesse Chessum of Shoreditch, it was a spectacular example of High Victorian Gothic, although relatively simple in detail and modest in materials. It had a centralized plan based on a Greek cross, and rose to a square tower with a high pyramidal roof. It was built of red Suffolk bricks with Bath stone dressings and was faced internally with cream-coloured gault bricks.

Seats for 940 were provided on the ground floor and a gallery at the West end could take 266; side galleries to hold several hundreds more were envisaged but never added. As it was, the church was grossly over-sized. Morning and evening congregations in 1902–3 needed only half the capacity or less.

Highbury Quadrant Congregational Church in 1990

LONDON · MISSIONARY · SOCIETY

Only the ancillary buildings remain – a school hall, classrooms, vestries, caretaker's flat and the organ chamber. The church was pulled down in 1954, after a long history of structural failure which extensive remedial work ultimately failed to check. The cause was thought to be a spring washing away the clay beneath the foundations.

The school hall is an irregular octagon of alternate long and short sides, rising through two storeys – the upper level galleried – to a clerestory and pyramidal roof. Around the central area individual classrooms were formed by movable wooden partitions. The disused gallery floor is ceiled off.

The new church, seating *c*270, is not improved by being grafted on to the old school, which is thrown into an overbearing prominence it was not designed for. Externally plain, comprising a rectangular nave, short transepts and a blocky West tower with chamfered corners, it is brick built with copper-covered roofs. In style it could be described as Norman.

Inside, it has a slender concrete portal frame roof. Between the framing the roof is panelled with acoustic boarding and the walls plastered – intended dark red facing bricks proved too costly. The architect was Kenneth M. Winch of Hastie, Winch & Kelly and the contractors were C. Pitt & Son Ltd.

The new church was fitted out with light oak chairs and communion platform furniture by G. Maile & Son Ltd. One relic from the old church incorporated into the new is a stained glass roundel (the Smallwood Memorial) set in the wall over the platform. The 1950s stained and painted glass in the nave windows is by Clifford Rankin.

53 Elizabeth House

Hurlock (formerly Myrtle) Street N5
(former Congregational mission hall)

Elizabeth House was so named in 1952, when the former mission hall was opened as a youth club by the Federation of Soroptimist Clubs and the Save the Children Fund. The name was chosen in honour of the Queen and a prominent Soroptimist, Elizabeth Hawes.

There had been a Primitive Methodist mission on the site from 1870 to 1876, but the main hall, a long room built on to the rear of the premises, was built in 1885 for a Congregational mission. It is a very plain structure, brick built, with a slated iron truss roof. The architects were J. E. Goodchild & Son.

54 Former Salvation Army Citadel

Ronalds Road N5
(Citadel Buildings)

This was built in 1891 to the design of William Gillbee Scott. The main entrance is in Holloway Road but the principal front is to the side street. The style is slightly eclectic – a standard late

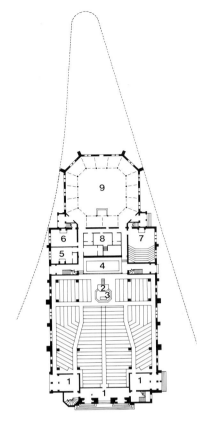

1 Vestibule
2 Pulpit
3 Platform and communion table
4 Organ
5 Minister's vestry
6 Deacons' vestry
7 Infants' room
8 Scullery, etc
9 School

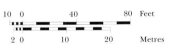

Highbury Quadrant Congregational Church (largely rebuilt). From a plan published in Congregational Year Book *(1881), and 1894–6 Ordnance Survey. (See illustration on page 124)*

(Opposite)
Highbury Quadrant Congregational Church. Detail of window dedicated to London Missionary Society

19th-century façade of orange brick, irregularly fenestrated, embellished with moulded bricks, Tudor-style oak doors, and a high jagged parapet with mock machicolation and a precarious-looking corner turret.

Along the ground floor are shuttered lock-up shops, small rooms with matchboarded walls and ceilings. They occupy the space beneath a large tiered gallery. Now disused, in the 1890s they were occupied respectively by a butcher, confectioner, boot-maker and greengrocer.

The gallery, the sides of which are partly hung with the kind of fretwork awning associated with railway platform buildings, looks towards a stage with a proscenium arch.

Damaged by bombing during the war, the Citadel was extensively renovated in the 1950s but closed c1963. The Holloway and Archway centres were amalgamated and a new Citadel constructed on the site of the old one in Junction Road (Gazetteer **73**). In 1989 plans to turn it into a Tibetan Buddhist monastery proved abortive. It remains a fabric warehouse, which it has been since its closure.

Citadel Buildings, Ronalds Road. Lock-up shops in 1990

55 St Giles Christian Mission

Bride Street N7
(former Arundel Square Congregational Chapel)

The present Baptist mission hall originated in 1863 as a Romanesque-style chapel, built for the rapidly growing district of Arundel Square. It was designed by Joseph James 'in conjunction with Mr. Phelps',[1] and built by a contractor from Penge, John Warne.

The shell of the building is of 1863, but its character is largely of 1934–5, when it was remodelled for the St Giles Christian Mission, founded in Seven Dials in 1860. It was lowered, given a contemporary-style entrance on Westbourne Road and refenestrated with rectangular windows to light a recast interior. The architect was H. Yolland Boreham of F. Boreham, Son, & Wallace.

Externally plain, it is brick built with Portland stone dressings and a hipped pantiled roof. There are two principal rooms rising through two storeys: a church and a lounge. The latter, intended as a games hall, incorporates the balcony front of the gallery of the old chapel, installed in 1866 by A. E. Harvey, a local builder. It is balustraded with ornamental cast-iron panels of curved section. The balustrade, and ornamental columns to support the gallery, were supplied by William Pedlar, a local gas-fitter and ironmonger.

The lounge is lit partly by lay-lights. To the sides are smaller rooms behind partly glazed partitions, used for prayer and meetings. The church, also lit partly by lay-lights, has a curved ceiling, suspended from a steel framework hung within the roof trusses, which incorporate some of the original timbers.

(Above)
Former games hall, St Giles Christian Mission, in 1990

(Left)
St Giles Christian Mission in 1990

The main entrance gives on to a vestibule and double staircase leading to the gallery (following the arrangement of the old chapel), which serves as a viewing platform and corridor giving access to the offices and other first-floor rooms. A deep basement, originally a school, contains recreation and community facilities.

56 Holloway United Reformed Church

Caledonian Road N7

Holloway Congregational Church (United Reformed since 1972) was built in 1959–60 to replace a ragstone Gothic chapel of 1848 wrecked by a land mine in 1940 (*see* Notes on Demolished Buildings). The congregation itself dates back to 1804, when a chapel was built in Holloway Place off Holloway Road (*see* Notes on Demolished Buildings). The church and school adjoining comprise two flat-roofed boxes of purplish brick, linked by a corridor. The church, smaller in plan but taller, has a large cross in relief in light brick and the corridor is decorated with a panel of masonry from the old building. A freestanding concrete cross nearby completes the ensemble. The architects were Diamond, Hodgkinson & Partners.

57 Caledonian Road Methodist Church

Caledonian Road N7 (corner of Market Road)

Built as a Primitive Methodist chapel in 1870, this is a handsome Italianate building of buff-coloured brick with orange brick decoration. It was designed by T. and W. Stone and built by William Goodman. The front is symmetrical, with four round-arched windows on the first floor, the ground floor brought forward the whole width to provide a vestibule. The doorway, behind rolling gates, is flanked by triple round-arched windows with cast-iron

Caledonian Road Methodist Church in 1990

92

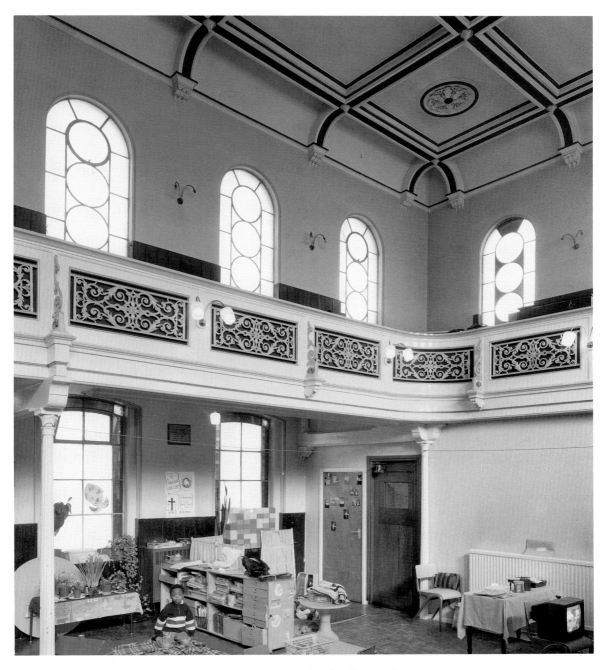

Caledonian Road Methodist Church in 1990

shafts. The main windows have cast-iron tracery in the form of three circular lights.

The ceiling is coved and coffered. There is a continuous gallery (the East end occupied by an organ), carried on iron columns, with an ornamental cast-iron front. It is an elegant interior, but there has been some partitioning beneath the gallery to provide rooms in connection with the use of the chapel as a crèche.

The basement schoolrooms, converted to offices, are used by London Borough of Islington Social Services.

Former Camden Road Baptist Church in 1991

58 Camden Road Baptist Church

Camden Road N7

Camden Road Baptist Church was designed by C. G. Searle and built in 1853–4. Oblong, with a pitched roof, it is Perpendicular in style, faced in Kentish Rag with ashlar dressings. The street front has a large pointed window above a central doorway, flanked by octagonal staircase towers (a gallery was installed in 1859). The gable has a high openwork parapet decorated with trefoils and a small pinnacle at the apex. The towers originally had spires but one was damaged by bombing in the Second World War and the other was taken down to match.

In 1989–90 the church was gutted and converted to a hostel and day centre for the St Mungo's Trust, by Craig, Hall & Rutley, architects. The congregation now meets in the former lecture hall behind the church in Hilldrop Road, built in 1858. Decorated instead of Perpendicular but otherwise matching the church, it comprised a large hall with a queen-post roof. It has been subdivided to form a church, with ancillary rooms behind on two floors. Several items from the old church have been reused, including cast-iron columns from the gallery and iron railings from the choir stalls.

59 Islington Arts Factory

Camden Road N7
(former Camden Road New Church)

This 'handsome Gothic edifice, with a lofty spire'[2] was built in 1873 on a lease from the City of London Corporation. It was designed by Edward C. Gosling and built by Perry Brothers.

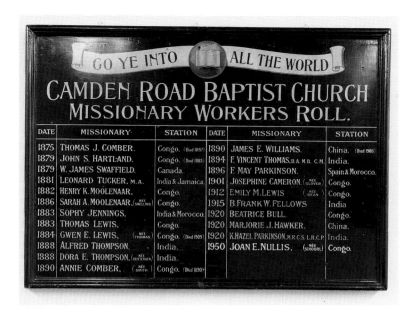

DATE	MISSIONARY	STATION	DATE	MISSIONARY	STATION
1875	THOMAS J. COMBER.	Congo. (Died 1887)	1890	JAMES E. WILLIAMS.	China. (Died 1908)
1879	JOHN S. HARTLAND.	Congo. (Died 1883)	1894	F. VINCENT THOMAS. B.A. M.B. C.M.	India.
1879	W. JAMES SWAFFIELD.	Canada.	1896	F. MAY PARKINSON.	Spain & Morocco.
1881	LEONARD TUCKER. M.A.	India & Jamaica.	1901	JOSEPHINE CAMERON. (NÉE GLOVER)	Congo.
1882	HENRY K. MOOLENAAR.	Congo.	1912	EMILY M. LEWIS (NÉE BEAN)	Congo.
1886	SARAH A. MOOLENAAR. (NÉE SNELLING)	Congo.	1915	B. FRANK W. FELLOWS	India
1883	SOPHY JENNINGS.	India & Morocco.	1920	BEATRICE BULL.	Congo.
1883	THOMAS LEWIS.	Congo.	1920	MARJORIE J. HAWKER.	China.
1884	GWEN E. LEWIS, (NÉE THOMAS)	Congo. (Died 1909)	1920	K. HAZEL PARKINSON. M.R.C.S. L.R.C.P.	India.
1888	ALFRED THOMPSON.	India.	1950	JOAN E. NULLIS. (NÉE SCHOORL)	Congo.
1888	DORA E. THOMPSON. (NÉE CRITTENDEN)	India.			
1890	ANNIE COMBER. (NÉE SMITH)	Congo. (Died 1890)			

Camden Road Baptist Church has been particularly active in promoting and supporting missionary work, both locally and overseas

Former Camden Road New Church (Islington Arts Factory). Staircase in Parkhurst Road building in 1990

*Former Camden Road New Church
(Islington Arts Factory) in 1990*

The Camden Road Society of the New Church (Swedenborgians) had moved from Cross Street, Hatton Garden. While the new church was building, they met in the Athenaeum adjoining, the site of which is now occupied by a service station. The congregation moved on to High Barnet in 1954 on the expiry of the lease. After some years as a youth club, the church became an arts centre.

It is in Early Decorated style, faced in Kentish Rag with ashlar dressings, and comprises an aisled nave with short transepts, apsidal sanctuary and Southwest tower. The church fittings have gone, and the stained glass has long been smashed. The interior has been partitioned into spaces for exhibition, work and storage.

Adjoining the church in Parkhurst Road is the former Sunday school and lecture hall, also by Gosling and contemporary with the church. The outside is drab, perfunctorily Gothic, of stock brick slightly relieved by orange brick stringing over the windows. The first-floor lecture hall, now a dance studio, has an open timber arch-brace roof.

The block was altered and extended in 1908 by Ernest Trobridge to provide a library for Swedenborgian literature, a caretaker's residence and a new entrance to church and lecture hall. Trobridge, son of the head of Belfast School of Art, was a member of the Camden Road Society. He later designed the New Church at Claygate near Esher (now demolished), and houses in Kingsbury, where he lived for many years.

The 'Verger's Cottage', faced in rubbed orange brick with a roughcast double gable, is a carefully detailed piece of Vernacular Revival, but the chief interest is in the church entrance hall and staircase, where the floor and dado are finished in predominantly green mosaic. The names of the rooms are picked out in red at the respective thresholds.

60 Sacred Heart of Jesus Roman Catholic Church

Eden Grove N7

Sacred Heart is one of a series of London churches founded by Canon Cornelius Keens. It replaced a nearby mission chapel dedicated to St Mary of the Angels, opened in 1855. The new church and presbytery, designed by F. H. Pownall, were built in 1869–70 by Messrs Carter of Holloway Road.

The church presents a high gabled street façade. This West front, with lean-to North aisle, large rose window and unfinished square tower, is linked to the presbytery by an archway with rooms over. The church, in Early English style, is built of yellow brick with stone dressings and moderate black-and-white brick ornamentation.

The interior is cool and dim, faced in dark red brick with black brick banding, and stone dressings including stiff-leaf capitals (by Farmer & Brindley) to the nave arcade piers. The nave is long and high with a clerestory and hammerbeam roof. Stained glass, some Victorian, some replacing that blasted in the Second World War, adds greatly to the overall effect. The sanctuary, formerly dominated by a Gothic high altar installed in the 1880s, was remodelled in 1960–1, by the architect A. Hodson Archard, of Archard &

Sacred Heart of Jesus Roman Catholic Church in 1990

Sacred Heart of Jesus Roman Catholic Church in 1990

Sacred Heart of Jesus Roman Catholic Church. Stations of the Cross and statuette of St Joan of Arc in 1990

Partners, with a plain green and white marble altar. The two side altars, and a gallery at the West end, are of the same date.

The Stations of the Cross, of oak carved in high relief and painted, are of 1909 by Anton Dapre.

Nearby in Eden Grove is the disused former convent and school of Notre Dame de Sion, a large L-shaped range, Italianate in style, built in 1874–5.

61 Holloway Seventh Day Adventist Church

Holloway Road N7

Built in 1927–8, this church was designed as a national Adventist conference headquarters and a permanent meeting-place for a congregation which had spent forty years worshipping in a succession of hired rooms and private houses. The architect was Samuel A. S. Yeo.

It is a showy building, resembling a cinema. Set behind a forecourt, it has a symmetrical façade in free Classical style, faced in brown brick with white rusticated dressings. The broad central bay is filled by a large round-arched window above three round-arched doorways, and is flanked by narrow staircase bays. The main window rises into an open pediment, above which is a high stepped parapet with volutes and a frieze of Classical ornamentation in relief.

Behind the façade is a vestibule opening on to a crush-room with cloakrooms, toilets and a pastor's reception room; on the first floor is a hall and gallery.

The church is a long rectangular room of double storey height. It has a curved false ceiling and is lit by tall round-arched windows along the sides and at the end. The East end has a platform with Gothic-style pulpit, baptistery and tiered seats for church elders, flanked by vestries. The body of the hall is fitted with blue plush tip-up seats; the floor is not raked.

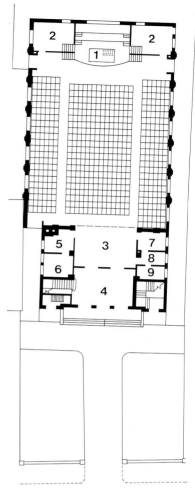

HOLLOWAY ROAD

1 Baptistery
2 Vestry
3 Crush-room
4 Vestibule
5 Ladies' cloakroom
6 Ladies' toilets
7 Pastor's reception room
8 Gentlemen's cloakroom
9 Gentlemen's toilets

Holloway Seventh Day Adventist Church. From a plan published in The Builder, *30 March 1928*

Holloway Seventh Day Adventist Church in 1990

62 Islington Central Methodist Church and Albany Hall

Palmer Place N7

Occupying the apex site between Palmer Place and Liverpool Road, this long flat-roofed range, slightly resembling a ship's hull, was built in 1962–3 as the new home of the Albany Mission, and the successor to the former Methodist churches in Liverpool Road and Drayton Park. Originally a Congregational venture, founded by Holloway Chapel, the mission became independent in 1891. It was based for many years in Albany Place, and in 1953 was taken over by Methodists from Islington Central Hall nearby, which had had to close.

The building, designed by Mauger, Gavin & Associates and built by H. T. Swaffer Ltd, comprises a church with a hall at the rear and ancillary rooms including living accommodation. It is faced in yellow and light brown brick with some weatherboarding. The church consists of an oblong nave seating 170, lit by high square windows (stained glass was installed in the 1980s) and a shallow top-lit chancel.

Islington Central Methodist Church in 1990

63 Roman Catholic Church of SS Joseph and Padarn

Salterton (formerly Gloucester) Road N7
(former Catholic Apostolic church)

This is a plain church, built of stock brick with sparse dressings of stone and orange brick, the West front pierced by five graduated lancets above a gabled porch with hipped lean-to extensions. It was designed as a Catholic Apostolic church by J. & J. Belcher and built in 1873 by William Carter of Camden Road.

In 1916 it became St Padarn's Church, replacing a temporary iron church set up nearby in 1909 in connection with the (Anglican) North London Welsh Church Mission. It remained a Welsh church until 1979. In 1982 it was bought by followers of the traditionalist Roman Catholic Archbishop Lefèbvre and rededicated.

It has a lofty aisleless nave with a semi-polygonal sanctuary ornamented with tall stained glass windows and Gothic-style panelling. The glass depicts St Padarn and the arms of the Welsh bishoprics and Canterbury. The West window, depicting SS Joseph and Edith, was acquired from an architectural salvage company. Furnishings include an octagonal pulpit matching the panelling and an octagonal stone font with a tall wooden cover.

A hall and a lean-to containing a sacristy and a confessional adjoin.

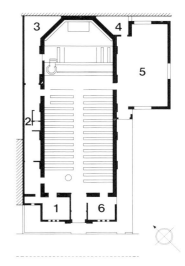

SALTERTON ROAD

1 Priest's room
2 Confessional
3 Sacristy
4 Kitchen
5 Church hall
6 Toilets, etc

Roman Catholic Church of SS Joseph and Padarn. From a survey made in 1991

Roman Catholic Church of SS Joseph and Padarn in 1990

101

64 Holloway Welsh Chapel

Sussex Way (formerly Road) N7
(Welsh Presbyterian)

Designed by A. G. Hennell, this modest Gothic-style chapel was built in 1873 for Welsh Calvinistic Methodists by Williams & Son of Thornhill Square. Alterations and improvements, including the installation of the galleries, were made in 1884 by a local architect, F. Boreham. Since then, apart from the loss of most of the original coloured glass in the Second World War, and the lowering of the high-level pulpit, little has been changed. A hall at the rear, designed by E. Francis Jones, was added in 1956–7.

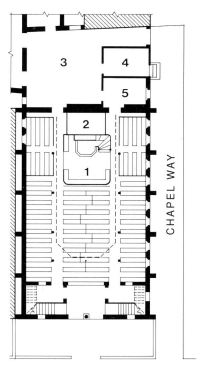

SUSSEX WAY

1 Deacons' seat
2 Organ
3 Church hall
4 Deacons' vestry
5 Minister's vestry

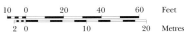

Holloway Welsh Chapel. From a survey made in 1991

65 Upper Holloway Baptist Church

Tollington Way N7

Upper Holloway Baptist Chapel, Holloway Road (*see* Notes on Demolished Buildings) was closed in 1977 and the site cleared in 1989 for a new church and Baptist Housing Association homes for the elderly and frail elderly.

    The new church, seating a congregation of 300–350, was opened for worship in June 1991. It forms part of the residential block, which has frontages to Holloway Road and Tollington Way. The architects were the Ainsworth Davey Partnership.

(This page and opposite)
Holloway Welsh Chapel in 1990

N19

66 Archway Central Hall

Archway Close N19

This was the last Central Hall built in London. Replacing a chapel of 1873 (*see* Notes on Demolished Buildings), and covering a much-enlarged site, it was designed in 1930 by George E. and K. G. Withers in limited competition and built in 1933–4 by C. P. Roberts & Co. Ltd. It comprises a block at the apex of St John's Way and Archway Close (formerly part of Archway Road) and a wing, containing the Main Hall, fronting St John's Way.

Shops occupy the ground floor of the apex block; there is also a small chapel, fitted up in 1988. On the first floor are offices, class-rooms and the Lesser Hall. The second floor contains further ancillary rooms. Additional accommodation includes a caretaker's penthouse flat and, in the basement, a gymnasium.

Archway Central Hall in 1990

A circulation area winds through the building from the main entrance in Archway Close to the Main Hall foyer. In the centre is a crush-room of irregular octagonal shape, known as the Octagon, lit by a lay-light.

Steel framed, faced in red brick and reconstituted Portland stone, the building is externally much like an ordinary retail and office development, but an Odeon-style skyscraper tower (now truncated) over the main entrance gave the building some architectural distinction. The cinema-like appearance was not accidental. The Methodist movie mogul J. Arthur Rank contributed to the cost of the building, the Main Hall of which was intended for film-shows and concerts as well as worship.

The passageways, staircases, Octagon and foyer are faced in predominantly cream-coloured tiles and have terrazzo floors. The Lesser Hall is a plain room of double-storey height with a shallow vaulted ceiling and a stage.

The Main Hall is a roughly horseshoe-shaped auditorium, originally seating 1,300, with a stage and organ at the narrow end and a gallery opposite. The ceiling is deeply coved, and has a large lay-light.

The organ was built by Wm Hill & Son and Norman & Beard, Ltd, incorporating the pipework of the organ from the earlier chapel.

The gallery remains intact, with original brown leatherette tip-up seats with wire hat-racks underneath, but the forward area of the hall has been cleared and the raked floor levelled for sports

Archway Central Hall. The Main Hall in 1990

Archway Central Hall. Corridor from the Main Hall foyer to the Octagon in 1990

use. The capacity of the hall has only been utilized of late for public inquiries into the Archway Motorway plan.

The curved area beneath the gallery was made into a new worship-room c1970 by Nye Saunders & Partners, architects. The wall behind the communion table is panelled with Cedar of Lebanon.

It was reported in 1989 that the Methodist Connexional Buildings Commission was in favour of the site being redeveloped as the administrative headquarters for the whole Methodist Church, but although this scheme has been abandoned the long-term future of the building is uncertain.

67 Replica House

Bavaria (formerly Blenheim) Road N19
(former Congregational mission hall)

Derelict for many years before conversion to commercial use c1960, this hall was built in 1883 for a mission (begun c1870) of Park Congregational Church, Crouch End. The architects were Lander & Bedells.

The street façade is a Classical composition in four bays, with pedimented entrances left and right (for GIRLS and BOYS respectively) and round-headed first-floor windows, rising to a high sham gable with a pedimented top. It is of yellow brick with red brick and stone dressings.

The hall itself, which has had a first floor inserted, forms a large rear extension.

68 Former Presbyterian mission hall

No. 7 Elthorne (formerly Birkbeck) Road N19

Built for Highgate Presbyterian Church in 1907, this hall was closed *c*1954 and used subsequently by the National Assistance Board and other governmental bodies. It was renovated and modernized in 1989 and is now occupied by the Islington African Project and the Anglo-Akanthou Aid Society.

Designed *gratis* by George Lethbridge, it is a two-storey Queen Anne-style building of yellow and orange brick, in five bays with an entrance wing at the side. The Boothby Road front has twin gables faced in moulded brick.

69 Hargrave Hall

Hargrave Road N19

Built *c*1908 as Archway Assembly Hall, Hargrave Hall, as it has been called since 1938, replaced a Brethren meeting-house demolished to make way for Archway Station.

It is a substantial brick building comprising a raised ground-floor meeting-room and semi-basement ancillary rooms. The gabled street façade is in three bays with a large round-headed window flanked by a smaller window and entrance porch. It is in a free, vaguely Classical, style and executed in smooth brown brick with stone and gauged brick dressings.

Now owned by the London Borough of Islington, it is used for community activities.

70 Hornsey Rise Baptist Chapel

Hazellville Road N19

The impetus for the building of the chapel in 1881 was the Metropolitan Board of Works' refusal to allow an iron chapel on the site to remain any longer. The congregation had been formed ten years before, worshipping in its early years at Duncombe Hall in Duncombe Road, the site of which is now covered by Elthorne Park.

The new chapel, designed by M. M. Glover, was built around the old to ensure a smooth transition from one to the other. It was, perhaps, a memory of this chapel within a chapel that suggested the 'Burbidge Memorial Chapel', a low-ceilinged room built around the central pews in 1948, in response to depleted membership and cold.

Hornsey Rise Baptist Chapel. Detail of North wall in 1990

By 1881 membership had reportedly risen from 75 to 500 – though only about a hundred attended the foundation-stone laying – and it was for 500 that the chapel was built. But by 1895 there were only 46 members. In that year the building, by then vested in the London Baptist Property Board, was renovated and a new congregation formed, but although attendance rose nothing like 500 seats were ever needed.

It is a Gothic-style oblong building of yellow brick with some red brick string-courses. The gabled West front is curiously small-featured, with a close-set pair of pointed windows and a rose window over, all with plate tracery. There is a (rebuilt) central porch.

The interior is spacious with a lofty hammerbeam roof. The pews and other woodwork are finished in light-coloured graining in place of the original dark varnish stain. Furnishings include a bow-fronted Gothic-style pulpit and an organ by Rest Cartwright.

Built on to the side is the former Sunday school, now called the Gregory Hopper Hall after a former pastor. At the rear, a lean-to contains ancillary rooms including an office and vestry.

71 St Joseph's Roman Catholic Church

Highgate Hill N19

St Joseph's, at the top of Highgate Hill, is one of the great North London landmarks. It is the third church on the site, which was acquired by the Passionists in 1858 – they moved here from The Hyde, Hendon, where they had been since 1848. A temporary church, opened in 1859, was replaced during the following three years by one designed by E. W. Pugin.

This second church was decorated in 1880 under the direction of the architect Albert Vicars. Meanwhile, the monastery, St Joseph's Retreat, had been rebuilt in 1874–5 to house forty monks – it is an Italianate building, standing on a terrace overlooking London. The architect was F. W. Tasker.

The present church, designed by Vicars, was built on to the monastery in 1887–9 as the Memorial Church of the Sacerdotal Jubilee of Pope Leo XIII. It dominates the rise with an octagonal lantern and green dome. It is Romanesque in style and comprises an aisled rectangular nave, deep sanctuary with side chapels to the Sacred Heart and St Paul of the Cross (founder of the Passionists) and a Lady Chapel. The nave is broad with a shallow barrel-vaulted ceiling; the processional aisles are low and narrow. In the

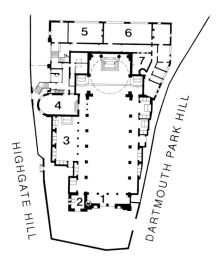

1 Narthex, organ loft over
2 Baptistery
3 Lady Chapel
4 Sacristy
5 Library
6 Refectory
7 Yard

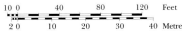

St Joseph's Roman Catholic Church and Retreat, showing original internal arrangement. From a plan published in Building News, *13 September 1889*

St Joseph's Roman Catholic Church in 1907. Photograph by G. Wills, Islington Central Library

(Opposite)
St Joseph's Roman Catholic Church.
Sanctuary in 1990

(Top left)
St Joseph's Roman Catholic Church in
1990

(Below left)
St Joseph's Roman Catholic Church.
Capital in North nave arcade in 1990

absence of transepts, the lantern rises above the sanctuary instead of a crossing. At the West end is a narthex with an organ gallery over, and a corner tower containing a baptistery and rising to a domed hexagonal upper stage.

The pier capitals of the nave arcades, and those beneath the organ gallery, are carved with motifs including the symbols of the Passion and musical instruments. The nave ceiling was painted by N. H. J. Westlake to illustrate the *Te Deum*. He also painted the panels above the nave arcades, depicting the mysteries of the Rosary.

The high altar and baldacchino, by Sharp & Ryan of Dublin, were erected in 1904 by Mrs Martha Lootens, in memory of the Revd A. Lootens (d. 1886) and Mr A. Lootens. A smaller altar was installed following the Second Vatican Council of 1964. This was replaced in December 1990 by a marble and sandstone altar, with matching ambo, designed by Gerald Murphy, Burles, Newton and Partners, architects, of Highgate. There is also an oak pulpit of *c*1937, an hexagonal structure on Ionic columns with a tester.

Former Junction Road Congregational Church in 1990

72 North London Spiritualist Church

Hornsey Road N19
(former Primitive Methodist chapel)

Built in 1908, this chapel was acquired by the North London Spiritualist Association in 1931. It is brick built with stone dressings and a pitched roof, in a simple Vernacular style. Inside it has dark timber roof trusses and matchboard ceiling. The wall behind the platform is decorated with a painted text from Psalms, ENTER INTO HIS GATES WITH THANKSGIVING AND INTO HIS COURTS WITH PRAISE.

73 Archway Citadel

Junction Road N19

This Salvation Army hall was built in 1968 to replace a Citadel opened in 1899 on the same site (*see* Notes on Demolished Buildings) and another in Ronalds Road (Gazetteer **54**).

Externally plain, it comprises ground-floor commercial premises (a bank) and a hall, lesser hall and ancillary rooms above. The main hall, trapezial in plan with a platform at the narrow end, has a steeply raked floor. It is lit by large tinted windows overlooking the street and is finished in shotcrete, with wooden panelling round the platform area. The architect was H. J. Wroughton.

74 Former Junction Road Congregational Church

Junction Road N19
(now Samaj Hall)

Junction Road Congregational Church, designed by W. F. Poulton, of Reading, was built in 1866 by Sawyer of Dulwich. Intended to seat 700, it originally had a cruciform plan comprising a long nave with short semi-polygonal transepts and large apse. An intended Southeast tower and spire were not completed. Faced in Kentish Rag with ashlar dressings, it is Decorated in style. The gabled West front has twin porches and a four-light pointed window flanked by two-light windows.

It was damaged by a flying bomb in 1944 and for some years afterwards services were held in the basement. Extensive internal remodelling was carried out *c*1952 by Houchin, Harrison & Stevens, architects. This involved dividing off the East end of the nave and realigning the church along the transepts, the South transept becoming the new sanctuary. The apse and greater part of the nave were subdivided to form offices, vestries and meeting-rooms.

Renamed the Church of the Growing Light, it closed as a place of Christian worship in 1978. Again remodelled, it is now occupied by the National Association of Patidar Samaj, a Hindu cultural organization.

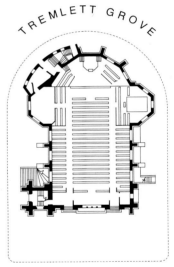

Junction Road Congregational Church. Showing general arrangement of seating prior to remodelling c1952. From a published plan by Houchin, Harrison and Stevens, architects (c1952) (copy in Islington Central Library), and 1894–6 Ordnance Survey

(This page and opposite)
St Gabriel's Roman Catholic Church in 1990

HOLLOWAY ROAD

ST JOHN'S VILLAS

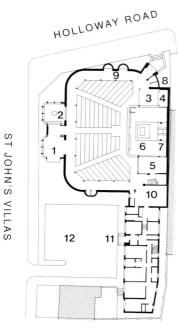

1 Vestibule
2 Baptistery
3 Choir
4 Organ gallery
5 Children's room
6 Altar
7 Tabernacle
8 Confessionals
9 Shrines
10 Sacristies
11 Priests' house and parish offices
12 Car park

St Gabriel's Roman Catholic Church. From plans by Gerard Goalen, architect (1965–6, Diocese of Westminster Parish Buildings Section), and plan published in Architectural Review, *May 1968*

75 St Gabriel's Roman Catholic Church

St John's Villas N19

St Gabriel's was designed by Gerard Goalen and built in 1966–8 by Marshall-Andrew & Co. Ltd. It replaces a temporary church in Hatchard Road, erected in 1928.

Brick built, with rounded corners, the walls are windowless to deaden traffic noise. They are broken on the West front by two linked pavilions of concrete and glass, also with curved corners, comprising a porch and baptistery. Twin semicircular projections on the North front contain shrines to Our Lady and the Sacred Heart. The roof comprises a flat concrete deck surrounded by a raised clerestory with continuous glazing on the inner, vertical, face and a sloping aluminium-clad outer face. There is a prominent concrete belfry.

The plan has some resemblance to many Nonconformist meeting-houses, being aligned on the short axis, but it is really that of a conventional rectangular church considerably foreshortened. The interior is faced in dark brick and has a dark stone raked floor. The dominating feature is the bare concrete roof deck, carried on slender piers round the edge.

The seating consists of wooden slabs on concrete supports, and the rest of the furnishings are similarly plain and simple. Two enormous fibreglass heads, patinated to resemble bronze, decorate the shrines. Of 'outstanding merit',[1] they were modelled by Willi Soukop.

Notes on Demolished Buildings

*Architects' names are in **bold**.*

Albany Place, Albany Mission
*Fl. c*1874–1961. Mission moved to Islington Central Methodist Church, Palmer Place (Gazetteer **62**).

Anatola Road, Primitive Methodist chapel
1883, replacing iron chapel. Closed 1936, in industrial/commercial use into mid-1960s.

Archway Road, Archway Road Wesleyan Methodist Chapel
Designed in limited competition by **John Johnston**. Built 1872–3 by Dove Brothers. Replaced iron chapel nearby, opened 1864. Latin-cross plan, utilizing kite-shaped site at apex of Archway Road and St John's Road (now St John's Way). Romanesque style, faced in light yellow brick with bands of dark malm paviours and Bath stone dressings. Gabled West front with triple entrance and large window over, flanked by staircase turrets with blue Bath stone domes. The original colour scheme was buff and brown for walls and dado, with blue panels with enrichments of red and blue, light brown roof timbers, white cornices and mouldings. The sanctuary was decorated with arcading and diapering. Dilapidated by mid-1920s, replaced by Archway Central Hall (Gazetteer **66**).

Barnsbury Grove, Barnsbury Chapel
J. W. Reed, 1862. Later Sandemanian chapel. Michael Faraday was a worshipper here. Closed 1901; the congregation moved to 3 Highbury Crescent. Site occupied by telephone exchange.

Barnsbury Street, Barnsbury Chapel
1835, altered 1841. Classical style, double-storey height, stuccoed. Pedimented front in three bays, round-arched windows each level,

Barnsbury Chapel, Barnsbury Street, in 1849 (demolished). Islington Central Library

lower outer windows over small porches with paired Doric columns. Sides with tall round-arched windows. Gallery replaced by side galleries 1848, by **John Tarring**. Schoolroom at rear 1850s, by Tarring. Closed c1903–9, later in industrial use.

Baxter Road, Baxter Memorial Chapel (later Salters' Hall (Baptist) Chapel)
(Congregational). **William Smith, junior**, 1862. Gothic style, brick with Bath stone dressings. Nave with transepts, small spired tower in angle. Galleried. Destroyed by fire 1981.

Birkbeck Road see *Elthorne Road*

Brewery Road, Belle Isle Baptist Chapel
Built 1878 for mission set up 1864 by Camden Road Baptist Church. Destroyed by bombing 11 January 1940.

Britannia Row, Congregational chapel
Finch Hill & Paraire, 1871–2. Mission originally established in Elder Walk by Harecourt Congregational Chapel (*q.v.*). Bombed 15/16 October 1940. Gothic style, with plate tracery.

Caledonian Road, near Bingfield Street, Congregational chapel
Andrew Trimen, 1850–1. Built by George Myers. Grecian style, with rusticated basement, portico and tall, narrow, round-headed windows. White Suffolk brick with stone dressings. Galleried.

Congregational chapel, Caledonian Road (demolished). Islington Central Library

Caledonian Road, corner of Hillmarton Road, Wesleyan Methodist chapel
Built 1866. Decorated Gothic style, faced in Kentish Rag. Rectangular nave, galleried; basement schoolroom. Southwest tower with broach spire. Seated 1,000. Closed 1915 and used as furniture repository. St Mary's Liberal Catholic Church 1926–76. Apse added c1926–30, by **Lutyens**. Demolished 1980 after community centre scheme failed.

Caledonian Road, Holloway Congregational Chapel

J. T. Emmett, 1846, replacing Independent chapel in Holloway Road. Decorated Gothic style, Kentish Rag with Bath stone dressings. Lofty aisled nave with arch-brace roof. Bombed 1940. Rebuilt.

Caledonian Road, north of Brewery Road, Presbyterian church

Barnett & Birch, 1855. Gothic style, ragstone-faced front between shops; 'wide and mean…No one could call this an attractive church'.[1] Closed 1868, reopened as St Matthias's CE Church. Chancel and South chapel 1883 by **William Smith**. Redundant 1978.

Carnegie (formerly Charlotte) Street, Wesleyan Association chapel

Built 1841 as United Methodist Free Church. Wrecked by land mine 1941; plans to build replacement on new Barnsbury Estate in 1950s abandoned.

Chequer Alley, near Bunhill Fields, Wesleyan chapel

E. Hoole, 1867. Plain building of stock brick with Bath stone dressings. The windows were set high up to deter vandals and exclude noise. Compulsorily purchased by Metropolitan Board of Works 1882.

Church Street see *Gaskin Street*

City Road, City Road Congregational Chapel

J. T. Emmett, 1850. Gothic style, rectangular aisled nave. Built for congregation founded 1848 and worshipping temporarily at Islington Green Chapel (Providence Place Chapel). Closed 1893. Demolished *c*1903/4.

City Road (corner of Oliver's Yard), Welsh Wesleyan chapel

Wilson, Son & Aldwinckle, 1882. Gothic style, rectangular plan, windows with plate tracery. Bombed *c*1940. Site occupied by Companies House.

Colebrooke Row (formerly River Terrace), Scottish Presbyterian church

Richard Dixon, 1834. Built, with a house on each side, for congregation formerly meeting at Chadwell Street Chapel (now Angel Baptist Church). Gothic style, brick with stone/stucco dressings. Symmetrical façade in three bays, central doorway and triple lancet window over, pointed windows on ground and first floors either side. Islington Presbyterian Church from 1867. Closed 1923. Became Albemarle Hall (billiards hall); antiques warehouse in 1960s and 1970s.

Compton Terrace, Union Chapel

Built 1806. Architect probably **Jacob Leroux**, original developer of Compton Terrace, or **William Wickings**, a surveyor employed in 1815 and 1823 to survey and repair the chapel.

Classical style, flanked by contemporary houses. Stucco and Portland stone façade of five bays, middle bays brought forward and rusticated on ground floor, pilaster order and pediment above. Open-sided, rusticated cupola, rebuilt after *c*1823.

Rectangular plan with curved East end. Galleries supported by Tuscan columns, with Ionic columns above carrying a shallow vaulted ceiling. Gallery fronts panelled in mahogany, with biblical texts in gilt. Sanctuary decorated with gilt inscriptions, including the Ten Commandments. High-level pulpit, and desks for reader and clerk, made of mahogany and satin wood, 'without regard to expense'.[2] Vestry/lecture hall at rear 1850, by **Blackett & James**. Chapel remodelled 1861 by **Lander & Bedells**. Changes included addition of portico with giant Ionic columns across full width of front, and Italianate clock tower. Demolished 1876 and rebuilt (Gazetteer **19**).

Cornwall Place see *Eden Grove*

Cross Street, Cross Street Baptist Chapel
John Barnett, 1852. Gothic style, gabled street front faced in ragstone with Bath stone dressings. Galleried interior. Open hammerbeam roof, iron reinforced, collared at two levels, upper collar king-trussed, lower queen-trussed. Bombed in Second World War, rebuilt (Gazetteer **21**).

Scottish Presbyterian church, Colebrooke Row (demolished). Islington Central Library

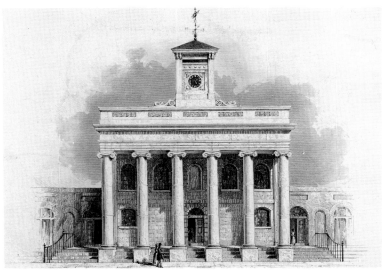

Union Chapel, Compton Terrace, as refronted in 1861 (demolished). Islington Central Library

119

Crouch Hill, Crouch Hill Presbyterian Church

Thomas Arnold, 1877 (lecture hall 1875–6). New hall and rooms at rear *c*1889. Gothic style, brick and stone dressings. Rectangular plan, gabled front, central doorway, two large pointed windows over. Three-stage Southwest tower with paired lancets on upper stages and short spire. Closed 1961.

Crouch Hill, Holly Park Wesleyan Methodist Church

E. Hoole, 1881–2. Rebuilt. Lecture hall/Sunday school at rear 1886, also by Hoole, survives (Gazetteer **41**).

Despard Road, Highgate Hill, Unitarian Church

Arnold Seaward Taylor, 1885. Romanesque style, brick with stone dressings, gable front, central entrance, large plate-traceried window above, flanked by small spired turrets. Closed 1961, demolished 1962.

Drayton Park, Highbury Wesleyan Chapel

Charles Laws, 1857. Replaced small chapel in George's Road (*q.v.*). Decorated Gothic style, Kentish Rag with Bath stone dressings. Oblong nave with aisles, transepts, semi-octagonal apse. Northwest tower, tiled spire. Galleries in North transept and over vestibule for Sunday scholars; basement school and meeting-room. Demolished 1929 to make way for Central Hall (below).

Drayton Park, Islington Central Hall

Sir Alfred Gelder, 1930. Saucer-domed hall seating 1,500, with meeting-halls, club-rooms, billiard-room, gymnasium, etc. Main auditorium designed for use as cinema. Closed 1953, used subsequently by German Methodist Mission and Albany Mission. Burned out 1985 after disuse following failure of 'Women's City' project. Demolished 1987.

Duncan Street, Catholic Apostolic church

Stevenson & Ramage, 1834. Small Classical-style church. Almost completely rebuilt in Gothic style by **G. Truefitt**, 1858, with higher nave and addition of transepts and entrance lobbies. Carving by Thomas Earp. Closed 1962, burned out 1967. 'Angels' throne' acquired by St Peter's Church, Devonia Road.

Durham Road, Seven Sisters Road, Primitive Methodist chapel

Built 1877, replacing iron chapel, closed 1917.

Ecclesbourne Road (formerly New Norfolk Street), Wesleyan chapel

Registered 1829, sold to Anglicans *c*1837.

Eden Grove (formerly Cornwall Place) chapel

Richard Dent's 1805–6 survey of Islington records a chapel in Cornwall Place, near where George Street and Eden Grove now meet.

Eden Grove (formerly Cornwall Place), Roman Catholic Chapel of St Mary of the Angels

Opened 1855; replaced by Sacred Heart Church nearby (Gazetteer **60**). Site now covered by Willow Court.

Elthorne (formerly Birkbeck) Road, Ebenezer (Strict) Baptist Chapel
J. W. Reed, 1866. Very plain brick-built hall with round-arched windows.

Elwood Street, Primitive Methodist chapel
Built 1889, closed 1951.

Essex Road (formerly Lower Road and Lower Street), Lower Street Meeting-house, also known as Lower Street Chapel
Stood in Lower Road on the corner of Green Man's Lane. Built 1744 on sixty-one-year lease at cost of 'at least' £430, replacing house licensed for meetings by Independents in July 1743. First purpose-built meeting-house in Islington parish. Plain brick hall with pantiled roof, small vestry room forming wing at side. Oblong plan, pulpit and desk in middle of long side. Galleries on three sides added 1768, **Mr Dermer**, surveyor.

Alterations 1820–22 by **Mr Jenkins**, probably **Revd William Jenkins**. Large front extension 1820–1: stuccoed Classical façade in five bays, middle three pedimented, outer bays canted. Vestry enlarged and schoolroom built above 1822. Closed *c*1864, congregation moved to new chapel in River Place (*q.v.*). Site later occupied by Green Man public house, 144A Essex Road.

Lower Street (Essex Road) Meeting-house, c1769 (demolished). From plans in Greater London Record Office, N/C/10/2, 35 (vestry room not shown)

Lower Street (Essex Road) Meeting-house, as extended 1820–1 (demolished). Islington Central Library

Exmouth Street, Spa Fields Chapel
Built *c*1770 as a place of amusement, known as the Pantheon. Domed rotunda with galleries on two levels. Converted to chapel by Countess of Huntingdon 1779. Demolished for road-widening 1886, replaced by chapel in Lloyd Square (*q.v.*).

Fann Street, Jewin Welsh Church
Charles Bell, 1878. Early English style, Kentish Rag with Portland stone dressings. Oblong plan, galleried. Tower, slated spire. Seated 650. Basement schools. Bombed 1940, rebuilt.

German Evangelical Church, Fowler Road (demolished). Islington Central Library

Fowler Road, German Evangelical Church

T. W. Constantine, 1861–2. Decorated Gothic style, pale yellow brick with red brick arches, Boxhill stone dressings. The growing German population in the Islington area then numbered more than 4,000. Closed during First World War, subsequently in commercial use. Burned out 1958.

Frog Lane see Popham Road

Gaskin (formerly Church) Street, Islington Chapel (Calvinistic Methodist)

Built 1788–93; hardcore for foundations reportedly came from Clerkenwell parish church, then being rebuilt. Square plan, two-storeyed, gabled front in three bays. Rear addition built 1801 as School of Industry for girls. Replaced 1815 by chapel in Upper Street (q.v.). British School from 1817; St Mary's parochial school 1841–61; Bishop Wilson's Memorial Hall 1861–91; briefly skating rink, then factory. Demolished 1970s.

Islington Chapel, Gaskin Street, c1788–93 (demolished). Islington Central Library

Gee Street, Wesleyan Methodist chapel

Built c1840, later Baptist, then Christian Community.

George's Road (formerly George's Place), Wesleyan Methodist chapel

In garden of No. 2. Built 1837; closed 1857 and let to Quakers, replaced by chapel in Drayton Park (q.v.). Closed as Quaker meeting-house c1864, replaced by meeting-house in Mercer's Road (q.v.).

Glasshouse Yard, Aldersgate Street, Glasshouse Yard Chapel

General Baptist meeting-house, *fl.* 18th century. Rectangular plan. In the 1890s it was said that the chapel's 'foundations are traceable under a paper-hanging factory'.[3] The American founder of the South Place Society, Revd Elhanan Winchester, preached there late 18th century.

Golden Lane, Wesleyan Methodist Sunday school

Opened 1798; transferred to Radnor Street (q.v.) 1819.

Goodinge Road, mission hall

Built 1884 as mission hall of Camden Road Baptist Church. Closed 1919, let to Salvation Army.

Goswell Road (Spencer Place), Spencer Place Baptist Chapel
Fl. *c*1847–69; replaced by chapel of same name in Charles (now Moreland) Street (Gazetteer **11**).

Great Arthur Street, Baptist chapel
Fl. from *c*1871 to the 1930s.

Grosvenor Avenue, Highbury New Park, Park Presbyterian Church
E. Habershon, 1861–3. Eclectic style, basically Italianate, with tall, round-headed windows; Southwest tower with Gothic spire; pepperpot turret on Southeast corner. Entrance up steps, through balustraded Doric portico. Built of white Suffolk brick with Bath stone dressings. Galleried on three sides. Closed 1942.

Park Presbyterian Church, Grosvenor Avenue (demolished). Islington Central Library

Highbury Hill, Highbury Hill Baptist Church
M. M. Glover, 1870–2. Brick, Romanesque style. Gabled front with corner towers of unequal heights, one with tall pyramidal

spire. Oblong plan, with galleries on three sides and organ in arched recess at East end. Badly damaged in Second World War; closed 1953. Demolished 1958 and council flats built on site.

Highbury Quadrant, Highbury Quadrant Congregational Church
John Sulman, 1881–2. Rebuilt, school and ancillary wings survive (Gazetteer **52**).

Highbury Station Road, Welsh Presbyterian church
Iron church with cupola. Opened 1874. Used from 1882 as mission of Union Chapel, known as Union Hall. Demolished *c*1904.

Highgate Hill, St Joseph's Roman Catholic Church
E. W. Pugin, 1860–3. Rebuilt (Gazetteer **71**).

Holloway Road, corner of Tollington Way, Upper Holloway Baptist Chapel
Jasper Cowell, 1866. Classical style, faced in brick and stone/stucco, part rusticated. Projecting central bay with main entrance and trio of round-arched windows above, pediment with scrolly ornamentation. Rectangular plan with curved East end. Ornate plaster ceiling with domed centre proved acoustically bad. Roof partly opened and remodelled when chapel renovated and galleries and clerestory windows added 1872 (**W. Allen Dixon**, architect). School 1868, also by Cowell. Chapel enlarged 1881. New classrooms 1893. Ceiling collapsed 1977 and services held in hall at rear; demolished 1989. New chapel and homes for elderly completed 1991 (Gazetteer **65**).

Highbury Quadrant Congregational Church, c1900 (demolished). Islington Central Library

Holloway Road, Holloway Chapel

1804, destroyed by arson 1807. Rebuilt 1808 using fittings from Highbury Grove Chapel. Enlarged 1821, 1834. Stuccoed façade in three bays, pedimented, central entrance and round-arched windows, giant pilaster order with arcading over upper windows. Originally Independent; Church of Scotland 1842–1956, old congregation erecting chapel in Caledonian Road (*q.v.*); scout hall until demolition *c*1960.

Holly Park see *Crouch Hill*

Hornsey Road, Wesleyan Methodist chapel

1821. A 'pretty little building, nearly square, and of the old Methodist type'.[4] Rebuilt 1858 (below).

Wesleyan Methodist chapel, Hornsey Road, 1858 (demolished). Islington Central Library

Hornsey Road, Wesleyan Methodist chapel

Andrew Trimen, 1858. Mixture of debased Decorated and Perpendicular styles. Grey Kentish stone with Bath stone dressings. Battlemented corner staircase towers with pinnacles and spires. West gallery. Demolished *c*1950.

James Street see *Mallow Street*

John Street see *Wedmore Street*

Junction Road, Salvation Army Citadel
1898–9. Castellated style. Brick with stone dressings. Gallery on three sides. Rebuilt 1968 (Gazetteer **73**).

Lavina Grove, King's Cross, Bethel Chapel
Baptist chapel, *fl.* 1865–1928.

Leonard Street (formerly Tabernacle Row), Whitefield's Tabernacle
1752–3, replacing timber structure of 1741. Eighty feet square, utilitarian in style, with high pyramidal roof and lantern. Galleried on all sides, accommodation for 4,000.

In the words of one critic, 'The Tabernacle of Mr. Whitefield was a mass of architectural deformity, and his chapel at Tottenham Court-road little better.'[5] The Tabernacle was the prototype for the slightly smaller Tottenham Court Road Chapel, built in 1756,[6] and may have been the work of the same architect-builder, **Matthew Pearce**.

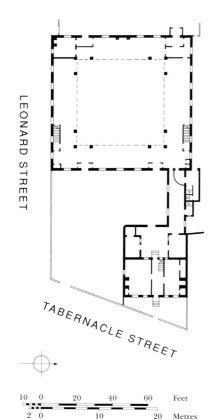

LEONARD STREET

TABERNACLE STREET

| 10 | 0 | 20 | 40 | 60 | Feet |
| 2 | 0 | | 10 | | 20 | Metres |

(Above)
Whitefield's Tabernacle and house, Leonard Street (demolished). From a drawing by J. B. Bunning on a deed dated 1844, in Corporation of London Records Office, Controller of City Lands, Deed Box 173, No. 30

(Top right)
Salvation Army Citadel, Junction Road, in 1899 (demolished). From a photograph in the possession of the Salvation Army

(Bottom right)
Whitefield's Tabernacle, Leonard Street (demolished). Finsbury Library

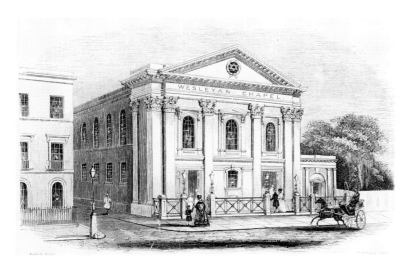

(Left)
Wesleyan Methodist chapel, Liverpool Road, c1827 (demolished). Islington Central Library

(Below left)
Wesleyan Methodist chapel, Liverpool Road, c1849 (demolished). Islington Central Library

(Below)
Wesleyan Methodist chapel, Liverpool Road (demolished). From a plan in Greater London Record Office, MBO 22 Case 861, and 1894–6 Ordnance Survey

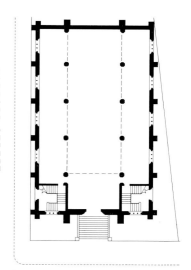

Liverpool Road, Wesleyan Methodist chapel

John Parkinson, 1827. Neoclassical style, front in three bays, giant Corinthian pilaster order. Destroyed by fire, rebuilt 1849. New building in Late Decorated Gothic style, by **James Wilson**. Lofty aisled nave, galleried. Closed 1929, congregation moved to Central Hall, Drayton Park (*q.v.*). Demolished *c*1932.

Lloyd Square, Spa Fields New Church

Lander & Bedells, 1885–6. Early English style, red brick with stone dressings. Centralized plan based on Greek cross. Galleried. Built for the Countess of Huntingdon's Connexion to replace Spa Fields Chapel, Exmouth Street (*q.v.*).

Lower Road and Lower Street see *Essex Road*

Macclesfield Street, Independent chapel
Fl. from *c*1872.

Maiden Lane see *York Way*

Mallow (formerly James) Street, Baptist chapel
Fl. 1862–*c*1900.

Mercer's Road, Friends' meeting-house
William Beck, 1864. Classical style, brick with stone dressings, rusticated brick pilasters. Front in five bays, middle bays open on ground floor to make colonnaded porch and rising to open pediment with round-arched window. Closed 1938.

Mildmay Park, Wesleyan Methodist chapel
W. W. Pocock, 1862. Decorated Gothic, Kentish Rag with Bath stone dressings, galleried. Gabled front with large central pointed window flanked by doorways with small pointed windows over, and corner staircase turrets. Seated more than 1,000. Apse and rooms added by 1890s. Sunday school/lecture hall at rear 1878, by **Charles Bell**. Closed 1964, used as warehouse, burned out while awaiting demolition 1973.

Mildmay Park, Mildmay Mission Conference Hall
Habershon & Pite, 1869–70. Large rectangular hall, Romanesque style. Shallow barrel-vaulted ceiling. Galleries on three sides. Deaconess House (1871) adjoined. Closed 1954.

New Norfolk Street see *Ecclesbourne Road*

Oliver's Yard see *City Road*

Packington Street, Methodist New Connexion chapel (Britannia Fields Chapel)
J. McLansborough, 1854. Built for society founded City Road, 1834. Early English style, brick with stone dressings. Rectangular plan with galleries on three sides. Three-bay gabled front with two doorways and three graduated lancets over; pinnacles each side. William Booth, founder of the Salvation Army, was minister 1854–61 and subsequently held Salvationist meetings here. Hall at rear 1932. Closed 1964 and council housing built on site.

Peel Court see *St John Street*

Pembroke Street (formerly William Street North, also known as Little William Street), Pembroke Street Chapel/Pembroke Hall
E. C. Robins, 1852. Brethren meeting-house. Brick built, rectangular hall. Stone-faced East (street) front, with porch. Buttressed sides. King-post roof. Closed *c*1948.

Pentonville Road, Pentonville Chapel see *Grimaldi Park House*
(Gazetteer **30**)

Popham Road (formerly Frog Lane), Primitive Methodist chapel
1854–5. First Primitive Methodist chapel in London. Closed 1897.

Queensland Road, Wesleyan mission
Fl. 1873–1922, became St Barnabas's Mission (Church of England).

Radnor Street, Wesleyan Methodist mission
School moved from Golden Lane (*q.v.*) to Radnor Street 1819; chapel opened *c*1870. Schools enlarged 1839, 1856, rebuilt 1881–3. Closed 1959/60.

Regent Street, City Road, Providence Chapel
Independent chapel opened *c*1850; rectangular plan. Closed 1903. Congregation moved to new chapel in Thane Villas (*q.v.*).

River Place (formerly River Street), Congregational church
Built 1863 to replace Lower Street Meeting-house (*q.v.*, Essex Road). Tall brick-built Romanesque-style hall. Lecture room at side built by 1872. Cinema *c*1908, later factory. Demolished between 1965 and 1978.

River Terrace see *Colebrooke Row*

St John's Square, Free-thinking Christians' meeting-house
1832. Tudor style, symmetrical gabled front in three bays with porch and four-light window over. Built for congregation originating 1798 as Universalist Church, set up 'as a protest against that awful doctrine of endless suffering, exalted into such prominence by the preaching of Wesley and Whitefield'.[7]

St John's Square, Wesleyan Methodist chapel/London Central Wesleyan Mission
James Wilson, 1849. Decorated Gothic style, gable front with large central window and twin turrets. Brick with Bath stone dressings. Refurbishment 1866, by **E. Bassett Keeling**. Three-floor Gothic-style extension *c*1898, comprising Sunday school, lecture hall, dispensary, etc, by **A. Wakerley**. Completely remodelled internally *c*1930. Burned out May 1941. Temporary reinstatement 1949. Proposed rebuilding abandoned; closed 1957.

St John Street, Peel Court Meeting-house
Meetings held from 1656 in Quaker carpenter's workshop. Freehold acquired by Friends 1692, the carpenter staying on as tenant. Enlarged in 1708, the 'old patched building'[8] was demolished in 1721 and a meeting-house built on enlarged site by **John Jennings**, a member of the meeting. In 1789 the ceiling was raised, piers supporting the galleries were replaced by thin columns, and windows facing St John's Lane were bricked up to cut out street noise. Cromwell described it as 'substantially built, with a characteristically plain interior'.[9] Square plan, two galleries; seated about 500. Closed 1926, used by Bedford Institute Association; bombed 1940. Name derives from old name of property, 'the Baker's Peel', referring to the long-handled shovel used in bakers' ovens.

St Paul's Road, Harecourt Congregational Chapel (United Reformed Church)
W. G. & E. Habershon, 1855. Replaced Hare Court Chapel, Aldersgate, City. Gothic style. Central plan comprising an octagon

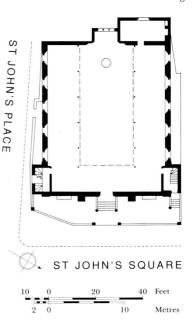

St John's Square Wesleyan Methodist chapel (demolished). From a plan in Greater London Record Office, MBO 22, Case 777, and 1894–6 Ordnance Survey

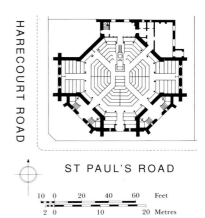

Harecourt Congregational Chapel, St Paul's Road (demolished). From published plan c1855 (copy in Islington Central Library)

129

Harecourt Congregational Chapel, St Paul's Road (demolished). Islington Central Library

with short arms along alternate axes, one arm forming vestry. Pyramidal roof. Galleried interior, altered 1908 by **George Carter**. Furnishings included 1864 Willis organ. Lecture hall built on to chapel 1870, by **T. Chatfeild Clarke**: Gothic style, rectangular plan. Mansard roof with ceiling of pointed arch section. Big quatrefoil windows at either end, pointed windows along one side.

Burned out 1982, stood in ruins until demolition 1989. New church on site (Gazetteer **34**).

Seven Sisters Road, Finsbury Park Congregational Church
C. H. Searle, 1882–3. Ancillary wing survives (Gazetteer **43**).

Shepperton Road (formerly Shepperton Street West), Independent chapel
Fl. from *c*1849; Methodist chapel *c*1854–9. St Bartholomew's National School from *c*1859.

Southgate Road, Trinity Presbyterian Church
T. E. Knightley, 1856–7. Site largely in London Borough of Hackney. Manse survives (Gazetteer **27**).

Spencer Place see *Goswell Road*

Tabernacle Row see *Leonard Street*

Thane Villas, Regent Street Chapel
Fl. 1903–*c*1947. Replaced Providence Chapel, Regent Street (*q.v.*).

Upper Street, Christadelphian hall
Brother Bosher, a Baptist converted to Christadelphianism 1868, 'built a good hall'[10] at the rear of No. 69 Upper Street. Disused before 1904.

Upper Street, Islington Chapel
Built 1814–15. Classical style, stuccoed. Front in four bays, windows and flanking doorways on ground floor with segmental heads, round-arched windows over. Fascia over middle bays;

square, domed turret. Alterations 1847–8 to West front: new porches and vestibule, turret raised and somewhat embellished, by **George Lamb**. Basement school added 1853, by **W. G. & E. Habershon**. Oblong plan, with galleries on Tuscan columns, organ on gallery at East end. Demolished for road widening, rebuilt on corner of Upper Street and Gaskin Street.

Upper Street, Unity Church

T. Chatfeild Clarke, 1860–2. Bombed 1940. Decorated Gothic style, Kentish Rag faced with Bath stone dressings and polished Aberdeen granite shafts to doorways. Square Northwest tower with octagonal spire. Nave with short, wide transepts and small semi-polygonal sanctuary. Side aisles with galleries over for schoolchildren. Fittings included an elaborate Bath stone pulpit, inlaid with coloured marbles and cements, carved by William Pearce. School and vestry adjoining built when congregation moved to Islington 1860.

(Top left)
Islington Chapel, Upper Street, c1847 (demolished). Islington Central Library

(Above)
Unity Church, Upper Street (demolished). Islington Central Library

131

Wedmore (formerly John) Street, Zoar Baptist Chapel
Built 1852, replaced 1887–8 by Zoar Hall, Tollington Park (Gazetteer **45**). Later called Wedmore Hall.

Wilderness Row, Wilderness Row Chapel
Opened 1785 by Welsh Calvinistic Methodists; probably older. John Wesley preached in a chapel apparently on this site in 1769. Enlarged 1806. Acquired by Wesleyan Methodists 1823. Replaced by St John's Square Wesleyan Methodist Chapel (*q.v.*) 1849; reopened as Zion Chapel (Strict Baptist). Probably rebuilt. Closed 1878. Part standing 1938, incorporated in commercial premises.

William Street North see *Pembroke Street*

Wilton Square, Salem Baptist Chapel
Built 1853 on lease from Clothworker's Co. Small Classical-style hall, front with rusticated porch flanked by tall round-headed windows. Closed 1913, later used by YMCA until 1962.

Wilton Square, Welsh Calvinistic Methodist chapel (Bethel Chapel)
Henry Hodge, 1852–3. Gothic style, rectangular plan, corbelled turrets on gable ends. Altered 1884, by **F. W. Boreham**. Closed 1955 and converted to hostel, since rebuilt.

Yerbury Road, Rupert Road Mission Hall
Searle & Hayes, 1887. Built for mission of Upper Holloway Baptist Chapel, Holloway Road (*q.v.*), started 1878 in Rupert Road. Closed before 1950.

York Way (formerly Maiden Lane), Battle Bridge Meeting House, also called Trinity Chapel
Built *c*1775; Wesleyan Methodist by 1807, later Particular Baptist. Converted to private house 1824/5.

Architects

(Professional qualifications shown where known)

AINSWORTH DAVEY PARTNERSHIP
  Upper Holloway Baptist Church, Tollington Way (1990–1)

ALDWINKLE *see* WILSON, SON & ALDWINKLE

ALLIES & MORRISON
  Grimaldi Park House, Pentonville Road (1990)

ARCHARD, A. Hodson (ARCHARD & PARTNERS)
  Remodelling of sanctuary, Sacred Heart of Jesus Roman Catholic Church, Eden
  Grove (1960–1)

ARNOLD, Thomas, FRIBA (d. 1912)
  Crouch Hill Presbyterian Church 1877 (lecture hall 1875–6) *Demolished*

ATTENBROW, W. B. (SPALDING, MYERS & ATTENBROW)
  Cross Street Baptist Church and ancillary buildings (1956)

ASHFORD, T. Murray
  Alterations, St James's, Pentonville (1933)

BARNES-WILLIAMS, FORD & GRIFFIN (Thomas Barnes-Williams, Lawton R.
Ford, Alfred Griffin)
  Alterations, new lecture hall, etc, Claremont Chapel, Pentonville Road (1902)

BARNETT, John (*see also* BARNETT & BIRCH)
  Cross Street Baptist Chapel (1852) *Demolished*
  Sunday School, Cross Street Baptist Chapel (1856)

BARNETT & BIRCH (John Barnett & William Cooper Birch)
  Presbyterian church, Caledonian Road (1855)

BATE, Stanley Chave KERR, LRIBA (1906–89) (WALTERS & KERR BATE)
  Roman Catholic Church of St Joan of Arc (1961–2), school (1961–3) and
  presbytery (1964)

BECK, William (1823–1907)
  Mercer's Road Friends' Meeting-house (1864) *Demolished*

BEDELLS *see* LANDER & BEDELLS

BELCHER, John & John
  Catholic Apostolic church, Salterton Road (1873)

BELL, Charles (d. 1899)
  Jewin Welsh Church, Fann Street (1878) *Demolished*
  Sunday school, Mildmay Park, Wesleyan Methodist chapel (1878) *Demolished*
  Restoration of Wesley's Chapel and Morning Chapel (1880)
  Manse, Wesley's Chapel (47 City Road) (1880)
  Benson Building, Wesley's Chapel (1880)

BENTLEY, Charles Joseph
  Providence Baptist Chapel, Highbury Place (1887–8)

BIRCHALL SCOTT *see* SCOTT

BLACKETT & JAMES (Walter Blackett & Joseph James)
  Vestry/lecture room, Union Chapel, Compton Terrace (1850) *Demolished*

BLAKE, John P., ARIBA
  Hall at Holloway Congregational Chapel (1938) *Demolished*

BLYTH, John
  Northampton Tabernacle, Amwell Street (1835)

BONELLA & PAULL (Alfred Augustus Bonella & H. J. Paull)
  Islington Chapel, Upper Street (1888–9)

BONEY, W. H.
Leysian Mission, Errol Street (1889–90)

BOREHAM, Frederick W.
(probably) Wesleyan Methodist chapel, Gillespie Road (1878); enlargement (1884)
Galleries, Holloway Welsh Chapel (1884)
Alterations, Welsh Calvinistic Methodist chapel, Wilton Square (1884) *Demolished*
Lecture hall, Wesleyan Methodist chapel, St John's Square (1887) *Demolished*
Entrance alterations, Wesleyan Methodist chapel, St John's Square (1889)

BOREHAM, F., SON & WALLACE *see* BOREHAM, H. YOLLAND

BOREHAM, H. Yolland
Remodelling, Arundel Square Congregational Chapel, for St Giles Christian Mission (1934–5)

BRADSHAW & GASS, of Bolton (J. J. Bradshaw and John Bradshaw Gass (1855–1939))
Leysian Mission, City Road (1903)

CAROE, Alban Douglas Rendall (CAROE & PARTNERS)
Jewin Welsh Church (1960)

CARTER, George
Restoration/alterations, Harecourt Congregational Chapel, St Paul's Road (1908) *Demolished*

CHADWICK *see* EMMETT

CLARKE, Howard CHATFEILD-
Preston Memorial Rooms, attached to Unity Church, Florence Street (1907)

CLARKE, Thomas CHATFEILD (1829–95)
Unity Church, Upper Street (1862) *Demolished*
Lecture hall, Harecourt Congregational Chapel (1870) *Demolished*
London Domestic Mission, Dingley Place (1877)

CONDER, Alfred, FRIBA (1845–1931)
Alterations, King's Cross Welsh Tabernacle, Pentonville Road (1904)
Claremont Institute, White Lion Street (1906 and 1910)

CONSTANTINE, T. W.
German Evangelical Church, Fowler Road (1862) *Demolished*

COTTON (probably Henry Robert COTTON or his father Henry Charles COTTON)
Alterations, Woodbridge Chapel School, Hayward's Place (1861)

COWELL, Jasper
Upper Holloway Baptist Chapel, Holloway Road (1866) *Demolished*

CRAIG, HALL & RUTLEY
Conversion to hostel/day centre, Camden Road Baptist Church (1989)

CUBITT, James, FRIBA (d. c1909)
Union Chapel, Compton Terrace (1876–7)

CURTIS, Robert L.
Blessed Sacrament Roman Catholic Church, Copenhagen Street (1916)

DANCE, George, the Younger (1741–1825)
(attributed) Wesley's Chapel, City Road (1777–8)
Wesley's House (front elevation), City Road (1779)

DAVIS, Joan
Conversion of crypt to community centre, Roman Catholic Church of St John the Evangelist, Duncan Terrace (1977–8)

DERMER, Mr
Galleries, Lower Street Meeting-house (1768) *Demolished*

DIAMOND, John (*see also* DIAMOND, HODGKINSON & PARTNERS)
New Court Congregational Church, Regina Road (1961)

DIAMOND, HODGKINSON & PARTNERS
Holloway Congregational Church, Caledonian Road (1960)

DIXON, Richard
    Scottish Presbyterian church, Colebrooke Row (1834) *Demolished*

DIXON, W. Allen
    Galleries and interior remodelling, Upper Holloway Baptist Chapel, Holloway
    Road (1872) *Demolished*

EMMETT, John Thomas
    City Road Congregational Chapel (1850) *Demolished*
    (As EMMETT & CHADWICK)
    Holloway Congregational Chapel, Caledonian Road (1845–6) *Demolished*

FINCH HILL *see* HILL & PARAIRE

FORD, *see* BARNES-WILLIAMS, FORD & GRIFFIN

GASS *see* BRADSHAW & GASS

GATLEY, G. H.
    Fifth Church of Christ Scientist, Blythwood Road (1962)

GELDER, Sir William Alfred (1855–1941)
    Islington Central Hall, Drayton Park (1930) *Demolished*

GILLBEE *see* HABERSHON

GILLBEE *see* SCOTT

GLOVER, Morton Meacher
    Highbury Hill Baptist Church (1870–2) *Demolished*
    Hornsey Rise Baptist Chapel, Hazellville Road (1881)

GOALEN, Gerard
    St Gabriel's Roman Catholic Church, St John's Villas (1966–8)

GOODCHILD, J.
    Alterations/additions, Vernon Baptist Chapel (1871)

GOODCHILD, J. E. & Son
    Hurlock Street, Congregational mission (1885)

GOSLING, Edward C.
    Camden Road New Church and Sunday School (1873)

GRIFFIN, *see* BARNES-WILLIAMS, FORD & GRIFFIN

GUNTON, W. H., FRIBA, FRICS
    Rebuilding of Large Hall, Leysian Mission, City Road (1953–5)
    Remodelling, Finsbury Mission, Moreland Street (1958)

HABERSHON, Edward (d. 1901)
    Park Presbyterian Church, Grosvenor Avenue (1861–3) *Demolished*

HABERSHON, W. G. & E. (William Gillbee Habershon and Edward Habershon
(d. 1901))
    Basement school, Islington Chapel, Upper Street (1853) *Demolished*
    Harecourt Congregational Chapel, St Paul's Road (1855) *Demolished*

HABERSHON & PITE (William Gillbee Habershon and Alfred Robert Pite)
    Mildmay Mission Conference Hall and Deaconess House (1869–71), Mildmay
    Park *Demolished*

HASTIE WINCH & KELLY *see* WINCH

HENNELL, A. G.
    Holloway Welsh Chapel, Sussex Way (1873)

HILL & PARAIRE (Finch Hill & Edward Lewis Paraire)
    New Church College, Devonia Road (1866–7) *(see also* WELCH)
    Spencer Place Baptist Chapel, Moreland Street (1868) Remodelled
    Britannia Row, Congregational chapel (1871) *Demolished*

HODGE, Henry, ARIBA (b. 1824/5)
    Welsh Calvinistic Methodist chapel, Wilton Square (1852–3) *Demolished*
    Congregational Chapel, Pentonville Road (1854)

HODSON RIVERS
  Harecourt United Reformed Church, St Paul's Road (begun 1991)

HOOLE, Elijah (d. 1912)
  Wesleyan chapel, Chequer Alley (1867) *Demolished*
  Holly Park Wesleyan Methodist Church, Crouch Hill (1881–2), *demolished*, and Sunday school (1886)
  Restoration and alterations, Wesley's Chapel, City Road (1891)
  Restoration, Wesley's House, City Road (1897–8)

HOUCHIN, HARRISON & STEVENS
  Internal remodelling, Junction Road Congregational Church (1952)

HOYLAND, E. Douglas
  Spurgeon Memorial Baptist Chapel, Tollington Park (1908–9)

HURST, Aaron Henry (1762–99)
  Pentonville Chapel, Pentonville Road (1787–8) *Demolished*

JAMES, Joseph
  Arundel Square Congregational Chapel (1861–3) Remodelled

JAMES *see* BLACKETT & JAMES

JENKINS, Mr (probably The Revd William)
  Additions, Lower Street Meeting-house (1820–1, 1822) *Demolished*

JENKINS, The Revd William (*c*1763–1844)
  Alterations and additions, Wesley's Chapel, City Road, from *c*1810

JENKINS, J.
  Monuments to Joseph Benson (1749–1821), Adam Clarke (?1762–1832) and Richard Watson (1781–1833), Wesley's Chapel, City Road

JENNINGS, John
  Peel Court Meeting House, St John Street (1721) *Demolished*

JOHNSTON, John
  Archway Road Wesleyan Methodist Chapel (1872–3) *Demolished*

JONES, E. Francis
  Hall, Holloway Welsh Chapel, Sussex Way (1956–7)

KEELING, E. BASSETT (1836–86)
  Refurbishment, Wesleyan Methodist chapel, St John's Square (1866) *Demolished*

KERR BATE *see* BATE

KNIGHTLEY, Thomas Edward, FRIBA (1823–1905)
  Trinity Presbyterian Church, Southgate Road, Hackney (1856–7) *Demolished*
  Manse, Northchurch Road (1858)

LAMB, George
  Alterations, Islington Chapel, Upper Street, 1847–8 *Demolished*

LANDER *see* LANDER & BEDELLS

LANDER & BEDELLS (Richard Smith Lander and Charles King Bedells (*c*1832–97))
  Congregational chapel, Offord Road (1856–7)
  Remodelling, Union Chapel, Compton Terrace (1861) *Demolished*
  Congregational mission hall, Bavaria Road (1883)
  Spa Fields New Church, Lloyd Square (1885–6) *Demolished*

LAWS, Charles
  Highbury Wesleyan Chapel, Drayton Park (1857) *Demolished*

LEE, William WARD (d. 1883)
  Bunhill Fields Memorial Buildings (1881) Largely *demolished*

LEROUX, Jacob
  (attributed; *see also* WICKENS) Union Chapel, Compton Terrace (1806) *Demolished*

LETHBRIDGE, George
  Presbyterian mission hall, Elthorne Road (1907)

LUTYENS, Sir Edwin Landseer OM, KCIE, PRA (1869–1944)
Apse, St Mary's Liberal Catholic Church, Caledonian Road/Hillmarton Road
(c1926–30) *Demolished*

MANGAN, Wilfred Clarence, LRIBA, of Preston, Lancashire (d.1968)
Roman Catholic Church of Our Lady and St Joseph, Ball's Pond Road (1962–4)

MAUGER, GAVIN & ASSOCIATES
Islington Central Methodist Church, Palmer Place (1962)

McLANSBOROUGH, J., of Otley
Packington Street Methodist Chapel/Britannia Fields Chapel (1854) *Demolished*

MURPHY, Gerald, BURLES, NEWTON & PARTNERS
Decoration and reordering of St Joseph's Roman Catholic Church, Highgate Hill
(begun 1990)

NYE SAUNDERS & PARTNERS
Worship room, Archway Central Hall (c1970)

OWEN, Henry
Alterations, Claremont Chapel, Pentonville Road (1854)

PARAIRE *see* HILL & PARAIRE

PARKINSON, John
Liverpool Road Wesleyan Methodist Chapel (1827) Rebuilt, *demolished*

PARSONS, Henry
Finsbury Park Room, Blackstock Road (1879)

PAULL *see* BONELLA & PAULL

PAYNE, Alexander
Reredos, New Church College Chapel, Devonia Road (1879)

PIPE, Michael
Holly Park Methodist Church, Crouch Hill (1962)

PITE, Alfred Robert *see* HABERSHON & PITE

PITE, Arthur Beresford (1861–1934)
Paget Memorial Mission Hall, Randell's Road (1910)

POCOCK, William Wilmer (1813–99)
Mildmay Park Wesleyan Methodist Chapel (1862) *Demolished*
Various works, Wesley's Chapel, City Road, from 1850, including new vestries,
1860

PORRI, Arthur C. (of HOBDEN & PORRI) *see* WRIGHT, Herbert A.

POULTON, William Ford (of POULTON & WOODMAN) (c1820–1900)
Junction Road Congregational Church (1866)

POWNALL, Frederick Hyde
Sacred Heart of Jesus Roman Catholic Church, Eden Grove (1869–70)

PUGIN, Edward Welby (1834–75)
St Joseph's Roman Catholic Church, Highgate Hill (1860–3) Rebuilt

RAMAGE *see* STEVENSON & RAMAGE

REDDALL, David G.
Monument, Highbury Wesleyan Chapel (1878) *Destroyed?*

REED, James Wesley
Barnsbury Grove Congregational Chapel (1862) *Demolished*
Ebenezer Baptist Chapel, Elthorne Road (1866) *Demolished*

ROBINS, Edward Cookworthy (1834–1918)
Pembroke Street (formerly William Street North or Little William Street) Chapel
(1852) *Demolished*

SCOLES, Joseph John (1798–1863)
Roman Catholic Church of St John the Evangelist, Duncan Terrace (1843)

SCOTT, T. G. Birchall
  Enlargement, Blessed Sacrament Roman Catholic Church, Copenhagen Street (1957)

SCOTT, W. Gillbee, FRIBA (1857–1930)
  Salvation Army Citadel, Ronalds Road (1891)

SEARLE, Charles Gray
  Camden Road Baptist Church (1853–4) *Interior remodelled*

SEARLE, Charles Gray & Son
  Whitefield Tabernacle, Leonard Street (1868–9) *Interior remodelled*
  New Court Congregational Church, Tollington Park (1870)

SEARLE, Charles Henry
  Finsbury Park Congregational Church and lecture hall etc, Seven Sisters Road (1882–3) Church *demolished*

SEARLE & HAYES
  Schoolroom, Cross Street Baptist Chapel (1883)
  Congregational mission, Lennox Road (1884) *Remodelled*
  Rupert Road Mission Hall, Yerbury Road (1887) *Demolished*

SEARLE, SON & HAYES
  Alterations & additions, Upper Holloway Baptist Chapel (1881) *Demolished*

SLATER, William (1819–72)
  Conversion of Rawstorne Street Chapel to National School (1855)

SMITH, William (jr)
  Baxter Memorial Chapel, Baxter Road (1862)
  Additions, St Matthias's Church, Caledonian Road (1883)

SPALDING, MYERS & ATTENBROW *see* ATTENBROW

STEVENSON & RAMAGE
  Catholic Apostolic Church, Duncan Street (1834) *Remodelled, demolished*

STONE, Thomas & William
  Primitive Methodist chapel, Caledonian Road (1870)

SULMAN, John
  Highbury Quadrant Congregational Church, lecture hall and ancillary buildings (1881–2) *Church rebuilt*

SWAINE, Edmund E., LRIBA
  Manse, Vernon Baptist Chapel, King's Cross Road (1962)

TARRING, John
  Claremont Chapel District School, King's Cross Road (1847)
  Alterations, Barnsbury Chapel, Barnsbury Street (1847–8) *Demolished*
  Schoolroom, Barnsbury Chapel (1850s) *Demolished*

TARRY, Mr (possibly John TARRING (*q.v.*))
  Alteration, Claremont Chapel, Pentonville Road (1860)

TASKER, Francis W.
  St Joseph's Retreat, Highgate Hill (1874–5)

TAYLER, Kenneth, ARIBA
  Unity Church, Upper Street (1958)

TAYLOR, Arnold Seaward
  Unitarian church, Despard Road (1885) *Demolished*

TRIMEN, Andrew
  Caledonian Road Congregational Chapel (1850–1) *Demolished*
  Hornsey Road Wesleyan Methodist Chapel, corner of Andover Road (1858) *Demolished*

TROBRIDGE, Ernest George (1884–1942)
  Verger's Cottage and internal remodelling of Sunday school, Parkhurst Road, ancillary to Camden Road New Church (1908)

TRUEFITT, George (1824–1902)
Remodelling, Catholic Apostolic church, Duncan Street (1858) *Demolished*

VICARS, Alfred (1840–96)
St Joseph's Roman Catholic Church, Highgate Hill (1887–9)

WAKERLEY, A., of Leicester
Additions, etc, St John's Square Wesleyan Methodist chapel (1898) *Demolished*

WALLEN (probably William)
Claremont Chapel, Pentonville Road (1819)

WALTERS & KERR BATE *see* BATE

WARD LEE *see* LEE

WELCH, Edward (1806–68)
North wing, New Church College, Devonia Road (1852) Altered

WHEAL, Francis & Partners
Proposed rebuilding, Blessed Sacrament Roman Catholic Church, Copenhagen Street (1990/1)

WHIDDINGTON, William
Alterations, Offord Road Congregational Chapel (1905)

WHITE, K. C. & PARTNERS
Church Hall, Tollington Park Baptist Church (1972)

WICKENS, William (?William Wickings)
Surveyor employed 1815, 1823, to survey and supervise repairs, Union Chapel, Compton Terrace; possibly original architect

WICKINGS *see* WICKENS

WILKINSON, Trevor (TREVOR WILKINSON ASSOCIATES)
Restoration, Wesley's Chapel, City Road (1973–8)

WILLIAMS, *see* BARNES-WILLIAMS, FORD & GRIFFIN

WILSON, James (1816–1900), of Bath
Liverpool Road Wesleyan Methodist Chapel (1849) *Demolished*
St John's Square Wesleyan Methodist Chapel (1849) *Demolished*

WILSON, SON & ALDWINCKLE (Andrew Wilson and T. W. Aldwinckle, FRIBA, d. 1920)
Welsh Wesleyan Methodist Chapel, City Road (1882) *Demolished*

WINCH, Kenneth M., MBE, FRIBA
Highbury Quadrant Congregational Church (1957)

WITHERS, George E. (1874–1945) & K. G., FFRIBA
Archway Central Hall, Archway Close (1934)

WRIGHT, Herbert A., FSI
Restoration, Highbury Quadrant Congregational Church, with Arthur C. PORRI, FRIBA, of HOBDEN & PORRI (1928–30)
Mount Zion Chapel School, Arlington Way (1929–30)

WROUGHTON, H. J.
Archway Citadel, Junction Road (1968)

YEO, Samuel Arthur Spear, ARIBA (d. 1966)
Holloway Seventh Day Adventist Church, Holloway Road (1927–8)

YOUNG, A. W.
Bethany Hall, Barnsbury Road (1934)

Glossary

Baptists
First Baptist church in England, formed 1611 by Thomas Helwys (1550–1616), gave rise to General Baptist movement, practising adult baptism. Particular Baptist movement, Calvinist in origin, denied communion to non-members, which rule continued to be enforced by the Strict Baptists after the union of the General and Particular Baptists in 1891.

Brethren
Fundamentalist Puritan sect founded in Ireland in the late 1820s by A. N. Groves, John Nelson Darby (1800–82) and others, and established in England at Plymouth; often still referred to as Plymouth Brethren. Split 1847 into 'Exclusive' and 'Open' Brethren.

Calvinistic Methodism see *Countess of Huntingdon's Connexion, Presbyterian Church of Wales* and *Whitefield*

Catholic Apostolic Church
Founded *c*1828–32 by the Scottish Presbyterian preacher and theologian Edward Irving (1792–1834), expelled from the ministry for heresy in 1833. The church, founded on Irving's charismatic personality and Apocalyptic visions, was initially Pentecostalist in character. After Irving's leadership was subverted an elaborately ritualistic liturgy developed.

Christadelphians
Millenarian, fundamentalist sect founded in the USA in the late 1840s by an Englishman, John Thomas (1805–71).

Congregationalism
The principle of self-government of an individual church by its congregation, deriving from the Lutheran doctrine of the priesthood of all believers, advocated by Robert Browne (*c*1550–*c*1633). First Congregational church in England founded by Henry Jacob (1563–1624) in Southwark in 1616. Congregationalist churches (formerly called Independent) have a strong evangelical tradition. *See* United Reformed Church.

Countess of Huntingdon's Connexion
Calvinistic Methodist sect, founded in the 1740s by Selina Hastings, Countess of Huntingdon (1707–91), a close associate of Whitefield and the Wesleys. Through Lady Huntingdon's social position, and her policy of building chapels in fashionable towns, the Connexion was influential in spreading Methodism among the upper classes.

Elim Pentecostal Church
One of two main British Pentecostal Churches, founded in 1915 as the Elim Foursquare Gospel Alliance.

Glassites see *Sandemanians*

Independents see *Congregationalism*

Irvingites see *Catholic Apostolic Church*

Jehovah's Witnesses
Strongly evangelical millenarian sect, founded in the USA by Charles Taze Russell in the early 1870s but not named Jehovah's Witnesses until 1931.

Liberal Catholic Church
Founded in London *c*1908. Highly ritualistic church, combining elements of Roman Catholic, Anglo-Catholic and Eastern Orthodox liturgies, but theologically distinct from these churches in eschewing the gloomier elements of conventional Christian eschatology.

Methodism
Evangelical movement founded 1738 by John Wesley and others, originally as a revivalist wing of the Church of England, but developing into a separate Nonconformist church by 1795. Successive rifts within the movement largely mended with the union of the principal branches as the Methodist Church of Great Britain and Ireland in 1932 and the formation of the World Methodist Council. Like 'Quaker', the term 'Methodist' originated as a somewhat derogatory nickname.

Methodist New Connexion
Group seceding from Wesleyan Methodists in 1797.

New Jerusalem Church (New Church)
Founded 1787 to follow the revelational doctrines of Emanuel Swedenborg (*q.v.*), who believed that he was the medium through which the New Jerusalem, foretold in the Book of Revelations, would be founded on earth.

Pentecostalism
Movement originating in the USA in the early 20th century, combining biblical fundamentalism with belief in the 'gift' of the Holy Ghost to individual members, manifesting itself in ecstatic, inspirational behaviour. The name refers to the descent of the Holy Ghost to the Apostles at Pentecost, the Jewish harvest festival. *See* Elim Pentecostal Church.

Plymouth Brethren see *Brethren*

Presbyterian Church of Wales (formerly Calvinistic Methodist Church)
The principal Welsh Free church.

Presbyterianism
System of government in Calvinistic churches, whereby the minister is one of a number of lay elders presiding over the membership of a local church, and representative elders constitute a 'presbytery' controlling churches regionally.

Primitive Methodist Church
Breakaway Methodist movement formed in 1811; merged with the Wesleyan and United Methodist Churches in 1932.

Quakers see Society of Friends

Salvation Army
Founded in Whitechapel in 1865 as the 'Christian Revival Association' by William (1829–1912) and Mrs Catherine (1829–90) Booth; name adopted in 1878. Strongly evangelical sect, deriving from Wesleyan Methodism, characterized by quasi-military rhetoric and style of dress, music, etc, and by indefatigable proselytization and social work.

Sandemanians
Religious community founded by John Glas (1695–1773), expelled from the ministry of the Church of Scotland in 1728 for his opposition to civil interference in church affairs and generally independent stance. The Glassite Church was spread to England and America by Glas's son-in-law Robert Sandeman (1718–91), becoming known there as Sandemanian.

Seventh Day Adventist Church
Founded in the USA in 1844 by followers of a Baptist preacher, William Miller, who had claimed that the Second Coming of Christ would occur in 1843. Adventists, who observe a Saturday Sabbath, believe in the imminence of a literal Second Coming.

Society of Friends
Founded c1650 by George Fox (1624–91) as a reaction against presbyterianism, characterized by the absence of ministry, sacraments and ritual. Meetings have no formal structure, but depend on spontaneous contributions from attenders as the 'inner light' moves them.

Strict Baptists
Baptists who adhere to the Calvinistic practice, deriving from the doctrine of predestination, of admitting to communion only those baptized in accordance with their Church's teachings.

Swedenborg, Emanuel
Swedish scientist, philosopher and politician (1688–1722), whose religious and mystical writings form the basis of the theology of the New Church (*q.v.*).

Unitarianism
System of Christian belief and practice of mid-16th-century origin, based on the acceptance of God as the supreme being and of Christ as God's messenger to man, but denying the doctrine of the Trinity. In the 19th and 20th centuries Unitarianism has moved further and further away from dogma and now accommodates a very wide range of beliefs.

United Reformed Church
Formed in 1972 from the union of the Presbyterian Church in England and the Congregational Church in England and Wales.

Practises the sacraments of baptism and communion and has ordained clergy.

Wesleyan Methodists see *Methodist Church*

Wesley, Charles
Brother of John Wesley; prominent early Methodist and important hymn-writer (1707–88).

Wesley, John
Principal founder of Methodism (1703–91).

Whitefield, George
One of the founders of Methodism and the leader of the Calvinistic Methodist movement (1714–70).

Abbreviations

CRO	Corporation of London Records Office
FL	Finsbury Library local history collection
GL	Guildhall Library, Manuscripts Section
GLRO	Greater London Record Office
ICL	Islington Central Library, local history collection
RIBA	Royal Institute of British Architects
SF	Society of Friends, Friends' House
URC	United Reformed Church Historical Society collection

Select list of sources

The most comprehensive account of places of worship in the parish of Islington is in *The Victoria History of the Counties of England: A History of Middlesex*, Vol VIII (1985). It includes addresses registered as places of worship at various times by the General Register Office and is arranged by denomination. However, it contains very little architectural information. J. Finn's *Churches and other places of worship in Islington* (thesis, 1978–9, copy in Islington Central Library) covers the whole London Borough of Islington. It is based mainly on the classified files of local cuttings and ephemera at Finsbury and Islington Central Libraries, which are an invaluable source.

For identification and tracing of places of worship, the *Post Office Directory*, certificates of registration of Dissenting places of worship (GL) and Ordnance Survey maps (various editions) were used.

Records consulted relating to individual churches and other institutions include those of: Blessed Sacrament Roman Catholic Church; Chequer Alley Chapel (GLRO); City Road Congregational Chapel (GLRO); Claremont Chapel (FL, GLRO); Scottish Presbyterian church, Colebrooke Row (ICL, URC); Corporation of London, City Lands Committee (CRO); Cross Street Baptist Church; Crouch Hill Presbyterian Church (URC); Islington Chapel (FL); Lower Street Meeting (GLRO); Metropolitan Building Office (GLRO); New River Company (GLRO); Radnor Street Schools (GLRO); St Giles Christian Mission; the parish of St Mary, Islington (GLRO); Society of Friends, Six Weeks Meeting (SF); Trinity Presbyterian Church (GL, URC); Union Chapel; Upper Holloway Baptist Chapel (GLRO); Wesley's Chapel (GLRO).

Other primary sources consulted include: District Surveyors' Returns (GLRO); Middlesex Deeds Register (GLRO).

For Roman Catholic churches, an essential source is the collection of Welsh Papers, compiled by the late Professor Stephen Welsh (RIBA).

Information on many individual architects is contained in the series of Biographical Files at the RIBA Library.

Information on a number of places of worship in Islington has been compiled by Christopher Stell of the RCHME as part of its national survey of Nonconformist chapels and meeting-houses (*see* Chairman's Preface).

Periodicals consulted include: *The Architect; Architectural Review; Baptist Examiner; Baptist Messenger; The Builder; Building News; Catholic Building Review (Southern Edition); Claremont Monthly; Congregational Year Book; The Earthen Vessel and Gospel Herald; Islington Illustrated Local History Journal; Intellectual Repository; New Church Herald; Proceedings of the Wesley Historical Society.*

Works on specific places of worship

Anon, *Union Chapel, The Story of a Hundred Years* (1899)
Anon, *The Pictorial History of Wesley's Chapel and its Founder* (Pitkin Pictorials, 1981)
Anon, *Remembering all the Way* (1950) [Providence Chapel]
Beck, W., and Ball, T. F., *The London Friends' Meetings* (1869)
Boyling, Percy J., *John Wesley's Chapel* (1942)
Champion, Oliver C., and Ballard, A. E., *The Years Between 1851–1951* (1951) [Angel Baptist Church]
Clarke, Basil, *Parish Churches of London* (1966) [Anglican churches]
Davis, V. D., *The London Domestic Mission Society* (1935)
Dixon, Lyall D., *Seven Score Years and Ten* (c1938) [Islington Chapel]
Edwards, George W., *The Quaker Burial Ground, Bunhill Fields* (nd)
Harland, A. G. L., *The Tabernacle in Moorfields* (1909)
Maher, Christopher A., SS *Peter & Paul's Church Amwell Street* (1988)
McMurray, Nigel, *The stained glass of Wesley's Chapel* (1988)
Martin, J. Henry, *John Wesley's London Chapels* (The Wesley Historical Society Lectures No. 12, 1946)
North London Mission, *The Opening of the new Archway Central Hall* (souvenir booklet, 1934)
Ogilvie, Bro. John, F.M.S., *St Joseph's R.C. Church 1815–1988* (1988)
Owen, W.T., *Capel Elfed* (1989) [King's Cross Welsh Tabernacle]
Parkhurst, K. W., *Souvenir of Centenary of Camden Road Baptist Church 1854–1954*
Pryer, C. A. Humpage, *Quakers in Holloway, History of Holloway Meeting 1858–1966* (1975, typescript, in Society of Friends Library)
Snell, Henry R., *History of St John's Square Methodist Church Clerkenwell 1849–1957* (1957)

Spoor, Ralph M., *Illustrated Hand-Book to City Road Chapel, Burying Ground, and Wesley's House* (1881)
Stevenson, George J., *City Road Chapel and its Associations* (1872)
Taylor, R., *150 Years Not Out* (*c*1949) [Union Chapel]
Telford, John, *Wesley's Chapel and Wesley's House* (1906)
Titford, Caroline, *History of Unity Church* (1912)
Welch, Charles Edwin, *Two Calvinistic Methodist Chapels* (1975) [Spa Fields Chapel, Whitefield's Tabernacle]
Woodward, Max W., *One at London* (1966) [Wesley's Chapel]

Other printed books

Bateman, Revd Josiah, *The Life of the Right Rev. Daniel Wilson D.D.* (1860)
Booth, Charles, *Life and Labour of the People in London* (3rd series, 1902)
Briggs, Martin S., *Puritan Architecture and its Future* (1946)
Colvin, H. M., *Biographical Dictionary of British Architects, 1660–1840* (1978)
Cooke, Harriette J., *Mildmay*; or, *The Story of the First Deaconess Institution* (1892)
Coull, Thomas, *The History and Traditions of Islington* (1862)
Cromwell, Thomas, *Walks Through Islington* (1835)
Cromwell, Thomas, *History and Description of the Parish of Clerkenwell* (1828)
Curnock, Nehemiah (ed), *The Journal of Rev. John Wesley* A.M. (1915). *Dictionary of National Biography*
Gray, A. Stuart, *Edwardian Architecture: A Biographical Dictionary* (1985)
Heasman, Kathleen, *Evangelicals in Action. An appraisal of their social work in the Victorian era* (1962)
Lewis, Samuel, *History of Islington* (1842)
Lewis, Samuel, *Islington As It Was* (1854)
Lewis, Thomas, *A Retrospect of the Moral and Religious State of Islington, during the last forty years* (1842)
London Central YMCA Places of Worship Research Team (Howard Willows, ed), *A Guide to Worship in Central London* (1988)
London County Council, *Minutes of Proceedings (1889–1965)*
Mearns, Andrew, *Guide to the Congregational Churches of London* (1882)
Metropolitan Board of Works, *Minutes of Proceedings (1856–89)*
Mudie-Smith, R. (ed), *The Religious Life of London* (1904)
Nelson, John, *The History of Islington* (1811)
Pevsner, N., *The Buildings of England, London (2)* (1952)
Pinks, W. J., *The History of Clerkenwell* (1881)
Read, Benedict, *Victorian Sculpture* (1982)
Rooker, John, *Islington's Centenary Missionary Story 1828–1928* (1927)
Rottmann, A., *London Catholic Churches, A Historical and Artistic Record* (1926)
Saunders, Ann, *The Art and Architecture of London* (2nd edn, 1988)
Taylor, Dr and Mrs Howard, *Hudson Taylor and the China Inland Mission* (1918)
Thornbury, Walter, and Walford, Edward, *Old and New London* (Popular edn, 1897)
Usherwood, Stephen and Elizabeth, *Visit some London Catholic Churches* (1982)
Vanderkiste, R. W., *Notes and Narratives of a Six Years' Mission, Principally Among the Dens of London* (1852)
Vickers, John and Young, Betty, *A Methodist Guide to London and the South-East* (1980)
Ware, Dora, *A Short Dictionary of British Architects* (1967)
Weinreb, Ben and Hibbert, Christopher (eds), *The London Encyclopaedia* (1983)
White, Winifred M., *Six Weeks Meeting 1671–1971* (1971)
Whitley, W. T., *Baptists of London* (1928)
Willats, Eric A., *Streets With a Story: The Book of Islington* (2nd edn, 1988)
Wyman & Sons (pub), *The Architect's, Engineer's, and Building-Trades' Directory* (1868)
Zwart, Peter, *Islington* (1973)

Maps

Baker, Edward and Benjamin, Plan of Islington & its Environs (1793) (ICL)
Booth, Charles, *Descriptive Map of London Poverty* (1889)
Dent, Richard, Plan of the parish of St. Mary Islington (1805–6) (ICL)
Goad, Chas. E. Ltd, *Fire Insurance Plan of London* (various editions)
London County Council, *Municipal Map of London* (1913)
London Topographical Society, *The A to Z of Georgian London* (1982)
London Topographical Society, *The A to Z of Regency London* (1985)
London Topographical Society, *The A to Z of Victorian London* (1987)
Ordnance Survey 5ft series, 1894–6 and other editions

Notes

Introduction

1 *The North Metropolitan and Holloway and St Pancras Press*, 18 September 1875.
2 R. Mudie-Smith (ed), *The Religious Life of London* (1904), 151–2.
3 *Ibid*, 148–9.
4 Charles Booth, *Life and Labour of the People in London*, 3rd series: Religious Influences (1902), Vol 1, 125.
5 ICL, Committee for managing Union Chapel, Minutes 1806–9, 10 November 1806.
6 John Rooker, *Islington's Centenary Missionary Story 1828–1928* (1927), 3.
7 Booth, *op cit*, Vol 2, 135.
8 Booth, *op cit*, Vol 1, 151–2.
9 *Ibid*, 134.
10 Places where cloth undergoing manufacture was stretched on frames.
11 CRO, City Lands Committee Journal, 18 March 1752.
12 Mudie-Smith, *op cit*, 147.
13 Booth, *op cit*, Vol 2, 132.
14 Booth, *op cit*, Vol 2, 139.
15 R. W. Vanderkiste, *Notes and Narratives of a Six Years' Mission, Principally Among the Dens of London* (1852), 50.
16 *The Builder*, 12 November 1859, 746.
17 Booth, *op cit*, Vol 2, 153.
18 Henry R. Snell, *History of St. John's Square Methodist Church Clerkenwell 1849–1957* (1957), np.
19 Mudie-Smith, *op cit*, 135–6.
20 Booth, *op cit*, Vol 1, 140; the story of Campbell Road is told in Jerry White, *The Worst Street in North London* (1986).
21 *Ibid*, 141.
22 Mudie-Smith, *op cit*, 136.
23 *Evangelical Magazine*, quoted in Anon, *Union Chapel The Story of a Hundred Years* (1899).
24 London Congregational Union, *The Bitter Cry of Outcast London* (1883), 4.
25 *The Builder*, 26 December 1863, 911.
26 Charles Booth, *Descriptive Map of London Poverty* (1889).
27 Harold P. Clunn, *London Marches On* (1947), 166–7.
28 F. H. Wrintmore, *The Salvation of London* (c1958), 39.
29 Finsbury Library, Islington Chapel Church Book (1867), 8.
30 Bessie Reynolds, *Loaves and Fishes* (1899). *See* Eric Willats' article in *The Illustrated Islington Local History Journal*, No. 16.
31 An example of co-operation between missionary work and the welfare state is the Clerkenwell and Islington Medical Mission at Woodbridge Chapel, where non-denominational services and a National Health Service surgery are held.
32 Quoted in Max W. Woodward, *One at London* (1966), 19.
33 Quoted in Thomas Cromwell, *History and Description of the Parish of Clerkenwell* (1828), 294.
34 GLRO, N/C/10/18.
35 Ritual orientations are given throughout with capital letters; geographical orientations are in lower case.
36 *Building News*, 9 March 1866, 145.
37 *Ibid*.
38 GLRO, MBO 517, Case no. 1707.
39 GLRO, MBO 80, 31.
40 Martin S. Briggs, *Puritan Architecture and its Future* (1946), 39.
41 James Cubitt, *A Popular Handbook of Nonconformist Church Building* (1892), 51.
42 A. W. N. Pugin, *New Catholic Church at Islington*, in *Dublin Review*, February 1842, 139–41; reprinted in *The Builder*, 1 April 1843, 98–9.

EC1

1 GLRO, Acc 2558/1/9, 280.
2 The portico is not shown on an 1824 plan of the new chapel (GLRO, MDR 1824/6/120).
3 CRO, City Lands Journal, 19 May 1784.
4 Nehemiah Curnock (ed), *The Journal of Rev. John Wesley A. M.* (1915), Vol VI, 133.
5 Howard Colvin, *A Biographical Dictionary of British Architects 1600–1840* (1978), 516.
6 George J. Stevenson, *City Road Chapel and its Associations* (1872), 548.
7 GLRO, Acc 2330/23/1.
8 *The Builder*, 3 July 1880, 31.
9 Subsidence had been a problem for years, due to improved local drainage which had caused the original timber foundations to dry out and so rot.
10 There is a frequently repeated but unlikely story, variously embellished, that these columns were made from ships' masts presented by George III. Stevenson (*op cit*) does not mention it.
11 GLRO, N/M/41/67.
12 *The Story of the Leysian Mission,* in *Claremont Monthly* (1906), 239.
13 The national office of John Grooms Association for the Disabled is now at 10 Gloucester Drive, London N4 2LP.
14 St Mary's was demolished in 1899 and rebuilt in 1903 on a new site in Eldon Street.

EC2

1 A. G. L. Harland, *The Tabernacle in Moorfields* (1909), 18.

WC1

1 GLRO, Acc 2558/NR/1/15/1, 311.

N1

1 In London Borough of Hackney. Formerly in civil parish of Islington and included because of its historical association with Islington.
2 Andrew Mearns, *Guide to the Congregational Churches of London* (1882), 27.
3 *The Builder*, 3 April 1875, 292.
4 Union Chapel, Church Minutes, 11 June 1875, Report of the Building Committee.
5 *Intellectual Repository* (1859), 343.
6 Pugin, *op et loc cit*.
7 *Ibid*.
8 The Brotherhood Church's old premises, a former Congregational church on the corner of Southgate Road and Balmes Road, Hackney, were the venue for the Fifth Congress of the Russian Social Democratic Labour Party, held in 1907.
9 Ian Nairn, *Nairn's London* (revised edition 1988), 152.
10 Anon, *Remarks on Ecclesiastical Architecture as applied to Non-conformist Chapels*, in *Congregational Year Book* (1847), 157.
11 *The Earthen Vessel and Gospel Herald*, April 1897, 128.

N5

1 In the London Borough of Haringey, corner of Seven Sisters Road and Wilberforce Road. Gothic-style church with tall spire, seating 1,000-plus. Built 1874–5; rebuilt 1959–61.
2 *Dictionary of National Biography*.
3 Union Chapel, Committee for managing Union Chapel, Minutes, 1806–9, 10 November 1806.
4 Thomas Cromwell, *Walks Through Islington* (1835), 301.
5 Quoted in *Islington Gazette*, 28 November 1960.

N7

1 *Congregational Year Book*, 1863, 344.
2 Edward Walford, *Old and New London* (1897 edn), v, 380.

N19

1 Stephen and Elizabeth Underwood, *Visit some London Catholic Churches* (1982), 76.

Notes on Demolished Buildings

1 Basil F. L. Clarke, *Parish Churches of London* (1966), 93.
2 Anon, *History of Union Chapel* (1837) (appended to Thomas Lewis, *A Retrospect of the Moral and Religious State of Islington, during the last forty years* (1842), 52).
3 Moncure D. Conway, *Centenary History of the South Place Society* (1894).
4 Anon, *One Hundred Years in Hornsey Road 1821–1921*.
5 *Congregational Year Book* (1847), 1556.
6 Enlarged in 1759–60, it was replaced in 1898–9 by a 'hideous and vulgar structure' (Martin S. Briggs, *Puritan Architecture* (1946), 36) and destroyed by bombing in 1945. The site is now occupied by the American Church in London.
7 *The Christian Freeman*, May 1871.
8 Quoted in W. Beck & T. F. Ball, *The London Friends' Meetings* (1869), 194.
9 Thomas Cromwell, *History and Description of the Parish of Clerkenwell* (1828), 114.
10 *Christadelphian Magazine* (1904), 468.

St Joseph's Roman Catholic Church, Highgate Hill. Sanctuary

National Buildings Record

The National Buildings Record (NBR), founded in 1941, is the principal national archive relating to historic buildings. It consists of photographs (currently numbering more than two million), measured drawings, notes and other material, and is constantly being added to. It is housed at the RCHME's London headquarters, Fortress House, 23 Savile Row W1X 2JQ, and is open daily to the public. Copies of all RCHME photographs can be purchased from the NBR.

*NBR file numbers for all buildings in the Gazetteer are listed (in **bold**) below.*

1 Roman Catholic Church of SS Peter and Paul, Amwell Street **77300**
2 Bunhill Fields Meeting House, Banner Street **77304**
3 Angel Baptist Church, Chadwell Street **77314**
4 Wesley's Chapel, City Road **77315**
5 Former Leysian Mission, City Road **77316**
6 Former London Domestic Mission, Dingley Place **77323**
7 Former Leysian Mission, Errol Street **77328**
8 Jewin Welsh Church, Fann Street **77329**
9 Woodbridge Chapel, Hayward's Place **77334**
10 St Joseph's Roman Catholic Church, Lamb's Buildings **77350**
11 Finsbury Mission, Moreland Street **77353**
12 Former Independent chapel, Rawstorne Street **77342**
13 Former Whitefield Tabernacle, Leonard Street **77352**
14 Vernon Baptist Chapel, King's Cross Road **77326**
15 Former Claremont Chapel District School, King's Cross Road **77349**
16 Roman Catholic Church of Our Lady and St Joseph, Ball's Pond Road **77303**
17 Former Maberly Chapel, Ball's Pond Road **77302**
18 Former Bethany Hall, Barnsbury Road **77305**
19 Union Chapel, Compton Terrace **77317**

20 Blessed Sacrament Roman Catholic Church, Copenhagen Street **77318**
21 Cross Street Baptist Church **77319**
22 Roman Catholic Church of Our Lady of Czestochowa and St Casimir, Devonia Road **77322**
23 Roman Catholic Church of St John the Evangelist, Duncan Terrace **77324**
24 Former Sandemanian meeting-house, Furlong Road **77330**
25 Former Gifford Hall, Gifford Street **77331**
26 Christian meeting-room, Islington Park Street **77345**
27 Former manse, Trinity Presbyterian Church, Northchurch Road **77354**
28 Former Congregational chapel, Offord Road **77355**
29 King's Cross Welsh Tabernacle, Pentonville Road **77358**
30 Grimaldi Park House, Pentonville Road **77357**
31 Former Claremont Chapel, Pentonville Road **77359**
32 Former Providence Chapel, Providence Place **77361**
33 Paget Memorial Mission Hall, Randell's Road **77362**
34 Harecourt United Reformed Church, St Paul's Road **77368**
35 Former Islington Chapel, Upper Street **77374**
36 Unity Church, Upper Street **77375**
37 Islington Claremont United Reformed Church, White Lion Street **77376**
38 First Born Church of the Living God, White Lion Street **77377**
39 Christadelphian hall, Blackstock Road **77307**
40 Former Fifth Church of Christ Scientist, Blythwood Road **77311**
41 Holly Park Methodist Church, Crouch Hill **77320**
42 Former Congregational mission hall, Lennox Road **77351**
43 Former Sunday school, Finsbury Park Congregational Church, Playford Road **77360**
44 Newcourt Centre (Elim Pentecostal Church), Regina Road **77348**
45 Zoar Hall, Tollington Park **77372**
46 Tollington Park Baptist Chapel **77373**
47 St Mellitus's Roman Catholic Church, Tollington Park **77371**

48 Former Wesleyan Methodist chapel, Gillespie Road **77332**
49 Former Highbury Grove Chapel **77337**
50 Roman Catholic Church of St Joan of Arc, Highbury Park **77339**
51 Providence Baptist Chapel, Highbury Place **77336**
52 Highbury Quadrant Congregational Church **77338**
53 Former Congregational mission hall, Hurlock Street **77344**
54 Citadel Buildings, Ronalds Road **77365**
55 St Giles Christian Mission, Bride Street **77308**
56 Holloway United Reformed Church, Caledonian Road **77309**
57 Caledonian Road Methodist Church **77310**
58 Camden Road Baptist Church **77313**
59 Former Camden Road New Church **77312**
60 Sacred Heart of Jesus Roman Catholic Church, Eden Grove **77321**
61 Holloway Seventh Day Adventist Church, Holloway Road **77325**
62 Islington Central Methodist Church, Palmer Place **77341**
63 Roman Catholic Church of SS Joseph and Padarn, Salterton Road **77363**
64 Holloway Welsh Chapel, Sussex Way **77364**
65 Upper Holloway Baptist Church, Tollington Way **77370**
66 Archway Central Hall, Archway Close **77301**
67 Former Congregational mission hall, Bavaria Road **77306**
68 Former Presbyterian mission hall, Elthorne Road **77327**
69 Hargrave Hall, Hargrave Road **77333**
70 Hornsey Rise Baptist Chapel, Hazellville Road **77335**
71 St Joseph's Roman Catholic Church, Highgate Hill **77340**
72 North London Spiritualist Church, Hornsey Road **77343**
73 Archway Citadel, Junction Road **77347**
74 Former Junction Road Congregational Church **77346**
75 St Gabriel's Roman Catholic Church, St John's Villas **77367**

Index